Impulse and Fire

Reset & Regulate:
Anger Management and ADHD

Dr. Yuliya Richard, PsyD

Contents

Chapter 3: The ADHD Anger Cycle—Identifying Triggers and Reactions 42

Chapter 4: The Role of Neurotransmitters—Dopamine and the ADHD Response to Stress. 56

Chapter 5: Why ADHD Anger Feels Different — Emotional Dysregulation Explained 69

Chapter 6: The Impact of Untamed Anger— Relationships, Work, and Self-Esteem 83

Introduction

It happened yet again.

James sat in the break room, the aftermath of his outburst still echoing in his mind. His coffee had spilled—barely a splash, nothing major. But in the moment, it felt like the final straw. He had slammed his fist on the table, barked at a colleague who offered help, and stormed out of the meeting like a storm cloud detonating across the office floor. Now, the embarrassment settled in his stomach like a brick. All he remembered was that the work allocation was unfair and that he had to make a point. The rest, as they say, was history repeating itself.

He always told himself he'd keep his cool next time—be patient, walk away, breathe, or state his case calmly. Yet the rage always crept up, sharp and unannounced, like a wave crashing before you see it coming.

And this was not just at work either. His relationships were fraying—his partner had stopped engaging in arguments, opting instead for silence and distance. His children flinched when he raised his voice. At work, people walked on eggshells around him. Worst of all, he couldn't explain why this kept happening.

James isn't a bad person. He doesn't want to be angry.

He is just exhausted from trying to keep it together while constantly feeling on edge, misunderstood, and out of sync with others around him.

Maybe you've found yourself in a place similar to where James finds himself.

Maybe you're reading this because, like James, you've had too many moments you regret—moments where your anger seemed to hijack your body and mind. Maybe you've noticed that your fuse is shorter than others', that your frustration seems to erupt out of nowhere, or that it lingers long after the moment has passed. Perhaps people have told you that you "overreact," or "take things too personally," or that you're "too intense." Secretly, you've wondered if you're just wired differently.

Anger is a normal, even necessary, human emotion. But when it becomes overwhelming, unpredictable, or damaging—when it begins to erode our relationships, sabotage our professional lives, and unravel our mental well-being—it's time to take a closer look. And this is especially relevant if anger is paired with patterns of impulsivity, distractibility, restlessness, or difficulty regulating emotions. In these cases, it might signal the need for deeper work on the self.

Most people who struggle with containing or managing their anger often ask themselves:

- Why do I lose control so quickly, while others seem to keep their cool?

- Why do I feel fine one minute, and out of control the next?

- Why can't I just stop and think before I explode?

- What if this isn't just a "temper problem"?

- Could there be something deeper going on?

For some people, these questions eventually point to a common, but often misunderstood, misdiagnosed, or undiagnosed underlying condition—attention-deficit/hyperactivity disorder, abbreviated as ADHD. We will go into what ADHD means in diagnostic terms a little later, but its connection with anger management can be understood from the following statistic: 70% of adults and 80% of children diagnosed with ADHD report difficulties in emotional regulation (Nigg, 2020).

If you've been diagnosed with ADHD, you may already know how complex and frustrating it can be. If you haven't been diagnosed, but have always felt like your emotional responses don't match the situation, or your brain runs at a speed you can't quite harness, you might have spent years blaming yourself, wondering why you just can't "get it together."

This book is for those who have felt ashamed after an angry outburst they didn't see coming. It is for those who've tried the breathing techniques, the self-help blogs, the umpteen promises to "do better next time," only to feel like nothing sticks. It is for those who've been told to "calm down" or "stop overreacting," but find it's just not that simple.

The most important thing to remember is that even if your anger feels unmanageable right now, you're not broken, weak, too far gone, or alone.

Science tells us how emotions like anger develop. Causes rooted in neuroscience, psychology, and developmental history explain why some people struggle more than others to regulate their emotional responses. For many people, especially those with ADHD, anger isn't just a behavior problem, but a neurological one.

Impulse and Fire: Reset and Regulate Anger and ADHD doesn't promise quick fixes. It's not a one-size-fits-all guide to becoming a perfectly calm person overnight or forever. But it does offer clarity on why anger shows up the way it does, why it feels so impossible to control sometimes, and why it might be connected to something you've never fully explored before.

What makes this resource unique is that it doesn't just teach you how to manage anger. It helps you understand the system behind it—the mental, emotional, and neurological mechanisms that fuel the fire. It bridges the gap between surface-level advice and deeper self-awareness. It draws from the latest research on ADHD rage, impulsivity, and emotional dysregulation.

Some things you can expect to understand after reading this book are

- why anger manifests differently for different people.

- how impulsivity and emotional dysregulation are often part of a bigger picture.

- the connection between childhood experiences, brain development, and adult emotional responses.

- how ADHD affects the brain's ability to manage emotions, and what you can do about it.

Apart from the science behind anger, you'll also find plenty of practical, research-backed tools and strategies you can apply to start gaining control over your reactions, improving your relationships, and building more peace in your life. Whether you've been officially diagnosed with ADHD or suspect that something neurological might be at play, this book can be a valuable part of your journey.

Before we proceed any further, let me clarify that this book isn't meant to substitute therapy, medication, or professional guidance. But what it can do is support you, giving you insight, hope, and a deeper understanding of yourself. As you begin this healing journey, we recommend using this guide along with our online course, Impulsive Anger and Rage Management, which is available on our website, impulsivity. com.au. The online platform also hosts many more courses on managing several impulse control problems like binge drinking and eating, overspending, out-of-control sexual urges, relationship repair, and chronic procrastination (Richard, 2022).

If you've picked up this book, it's likely you've realized something isn't working in your attempts at managing your anger outbursts. You may have recognized that something needs to change. Perhaps, you feel you're ready to understand your anger—and not just manage it.

Whatever your motivation for change may be, it is a brave start. With the right effort in the right direction, you can rest assured that change is possible and worth every challenge flung its way.

Chapter 1

Understanding Anger—The Science Behind the Emotion

Jordan is 32 and was diagnosed with combined type ADHD in his early adulthood. He is a graphic designer in a fast-paced creative agency.

It was a Tuesday afternoon, and he was working remotely on a tight client deadline. His inbox was flooded, Slack notifications wouldn't stop pinging, and the task he was focused on had just been changed for the third time that day.

Jordan's partner, Sam, walked into the home office to ask a simple question: "Hey, do you know where the keys are?"

Without even looking up, Jordan snapped, "Why can't anyone leave me alone for five minutes? I'm trying to concentrate here! Why don't you look for the damn keys yourself for once?!"

Sam, startled, backed out of the room quietly. A minute later, guilt started to sink in for Jordan, but the emotional fire was still burning. The stress from shifting expectations, lack of focus, and sensory overload had made that one question feel like a personal attack.

The constant notifications, time pressure, and the demand to switch attention rapidly had overwhelmed Jordan's nervous system. A hallmark of ADHD, Jordan's brain had gone from calm to furious in seconds. There was no gradual build-up— just an explosion. After the outburst, Jordan felt ashamed, frustrated with himself, and isolated. "Why can't I control this? What's wrong with me?" he thought.

From the two short scenarios we have used, it isn't difficult to identify the problems associated with rage outbursts.

Impulsive and explosive rage, especially when tied to conditions like ADHD, can have an extremely damaging impact on a person's life and relationships. In personal relationships, repeated outbursts often lead to a breakdown of trust. Loved ones may begin to feel unsafe, constantly on edge, or emotionally distant, unsure when the next blow-up might happen. What starts as a moment of frustration can leave lasting emotional wounds, making healthy communication and connection difficult. Over time, this could erode intimacy, increase misunderstandings, and trap the individual in a cycle of guilt, shame, and isolation, further distancing them from the people they care about.

In the workplace, such outbursts can damage reputations and limit opportunities. Colleagues may view the individual as difficult or unpredictable, leading to strained team dynamics, missed leadership roles, and even job loss. Productivity may suffer as emotional overwhelm derails focus and leads to avoidance of tasks or rumination over past conflicts. Career growth is often stunted not because of a lack of talent, but due to an inability to manage pressure or regulate emotions during high-stress situations.

Beyond relationships and work, unchecked rage takes a toll on physical and mental health, too. Chronic emotional reactivity keeps the body in a constant state of stress, increasing the risk of anxiety and depression (Hartman et al., 2019). Stress may, in turn, lead to heart issues, high blood pressure, and sleep disturbances (American Heart Association, 2020). Individuals who struggle to manage their emotions constructively often lack emotional awareness—they don't recognize their internal build-up until it's too late. Without effective coping tools or the ability to pause and regulate in the moment, even small triggers can lead to massive overreactions. Avoiding or suppressing emotions only fuels the problem, allowing anger to simmer until it inevitably explodes.

In short, explosive rage doesn't just affect the moment, but quietly and steadily chips away at a person's emotional well-being, self-esteem, relationships, career, and physical health. Learning to handle emotions in a healthy and constructive manner is essential for a balanced and fulfilling life.

What Is Anger? A Biological and Evolutionary Perspective

Anger is a deeply rooted, biologically programmed emotional response. It's not a flaw or a failing, but a normal and universal emotion, shared by humans across cultures and time. Renowned psychologist Paul Ekman identified six basic human emotions in the 1970s. Alongside joy, sadness, fear, disgust, and surprise, anger is one of the six universal emotions, recognized in every society (Cherry, 2024) through distinct facial expressions and bodily cues, such as furrowed brows, narrowed eyes, and a clenched jaw.

Anger as an Evolutionary Survival Tool

From an evolutionary standpoint, scientists believe that anger developed as a survival mechanism. In the face of threat, injustice, or frustration, anger triggers the fight-or-flight response—an automatic reaction that prepares the body for action. Heart rate increases, breathing becomes shallow, and muscles tense, gearing us up to either confront danger or escape it. In primitive environments, this response was crucial for defending territory, protecting offspring, or asserting dominance within social groups.

Today, while threats may be more psychological than physical, the biological wiring still remains. Anger can still serve an adaptive function. It can energize us to stand up against unfairness, motivate us to protect ourselves, or spur action when we feel wronged. However, when misdirected or chronic, it can become maladaptive and harmful.

Universality and Cultural Expressions

Despite cultural differences in emotional norms, anger manifests consistently across human populations. Children, regardless of their upbringing, instinctively recognize angry expressions in caregivers and adults and quickly learn to interpret them (Garcia & Tully, 2020). This suggests a shared biological blueprint for experiencing and recognizing anger, supporting its fundamental role in human behavior.

However, the expression and regulation of anger can be shaped by environmental and cultural factors. Living conditions marked by poverty, overcrowding, unsafe environments, or chronic stress often increase vulnerability to anger. When basic needs aren't met or individuals lack healthy coping strategies, anger may become a frequent and overwhelming presence.

Trauma, Biology, and Anger

There is also a strong link between trauma and anger (National Center for PTSD, 2022). Trauma, especially when unresolved, can impair one's ability to regulate emotions, leading to intense and disproportionate anger responses. The emotional brain becomes hypervigilant, interpreting even neutral situations as threats. In such cases, anger becomes a protective mechanism, shielding individuals from deeper feelings of shame, fear, or helplessness.

The Role of Personality and Belief Systems

While biology lays the foundation for anger, personality traits and belief systems shape how anger is triggered and expressed. People with a fragile ego, a heightened sense of entitlement, or an external locus of control may experience anger more frequently and intensely. According to Lewis's shame-rage theory, individuals who feel humiliated or ashamed often redirect that internal pain outward as rage (Hejdenberg & Andrews, 2011). When we cannot tolerate discomfort, ambiguity, or differing perspectives, anger can become a default defense.

Moreover, cognitive distortions like rigid "should" and "must" beliefs, a fixation on blame, or a thirst for revenge can amplify anger. The emotion is not just felt in the body but also shaped by thoughts and interpretations of events. Muscle tension, shallow breathing, racing thoughts, and impulsive behaviors like yelling or lashing out are all parts of this biopsychosocial anger cycle.

Not a "Negative" Emotion

Crucially, we must understand that anger, in itself, is not a negative emotion. It is neither dangerous nor unnatural. How we respond to or act upon anger determines its impact. If we allow anger to drive our actions impulsively, we may make choices that harm ourselves or others, damaging relationships, careers, and even face legal consequences. However, if we acknowledge anger without being controlled by it, it becomes a powerful ally in setting boundaries, asserting needs, and advocating for positive change.

You can think of it this way—anger in the passenger seat may not always harm you, but anger in the driver's seat may cause a fatal accident. When driven by anger, you may do and say things that will harm you and others, or regret later.

The Dual Faces of Anger: Adaptive vs Maladaptive Responses

Anger, often misunderstood and maligned, is a complex and powerful emotion. It can be a force for good, fueling courage, resistance, and transformation, or a force of destruction, tearing down relationships, reputations, and even one's sense of self. Understanding the dual nature of anger is essential for learning how to manage it effectively and channel it into healthy, constructive avenues.

Adaptive Anger: Anger as a Catalyst for Change

In its adaptive form, anger serves as an internal alarm system. It tells us that something is wrong—our boundaries have been crossed, needs neglected, or an injustice has occurred. When expressed appropriately, it can strengthen bonds and promote understanding. For instance, a parent who becomes angry when their child is mistreated can use that emotion to advocate fiercely for their child's well-being. Similarly, social workers, activists, and writers often draw upon empathic anger—anger, not from personal grievance, but from witnessing harm done to others. This form of anger fuels advocacy and social progress.

History is rich with examples where righteous anger served as the backbone of civil rights movements. Leaders like Martin Luther King Jr. and Mahatma Gandhi transformed their indignation into disciplined action. Their anger wasn't expressed in violence, but rather in a controlled, purposeful way that demanded attention and inspired change. When Rosa Parks refused to obey the government-imposed segregation rules in public transport and remained seated, she turned her anger into a potent tool for social justice. Women's suffrage, labor rights, and modern climate and environmental activism are all movements that took root in the soil of justified anger.

Maladaptive Anger: When Anger Turns Toxic

Not all anger is healthy. When it becomes frequent, intense, or misdirected, it becomes maladaptive. In this form, anger can lead to aggression, passive aggression, or even self-destruction. Rather than solving problems, maladaptive anger often creates more of them. It damages relationships, impairs work performance, and endangers physical and mental health.

Some individuals use anger like a drug. Though psychology or the Diagnostic and Statistical Manual of Mental Disorders (DSM-5) doesn't formally recognize "anger" as a potentially addictive source (Lovering, 2022), just as thrill-seekers chase adrenaline highs, people can become addicted to the physiological rush of anger. The release of endorphins and adrenaline during a rage episode (Murray, 2025) can feel momentarily empowering, especially for those who otherwise feel helpless or unheard. But like any high, it eventually fades. The aftermath often leaves behind guilt, anxiety, and depression, pushing the person toward further emotional volatility or even substance use as a replacement.

In such cases, anger becomes a maladaptive coping mechanism. When substances like stimulants are used, the lines between emotional and chemical dependency blur. Without the "fix," whether emotional or pharmacological, the individual may revert to habitual anger or lash out, seeking validation or support.

Forms of Unhealthy Anger

We tend to assume that anger can only manifest as violence. By violence, we mean physical violence against people and

Impulse and Fire

situations. However, maladaptive anger doesn't always explode outward in violent or obvious ways. It can be subtle and insidious. It may show up in the following:

- **Verbal abuse:** Harsh words, sarcasm, or controlling language.

- **Body language:** Clenched fists, tense posture, or threatening stares.

- **Inaction:** Using silent treatment or withdrawing affection as punishment.

- **Passive aggression:** Indirect hostility, like backhanded compliments or deliberate procrastination.

- **Self-directed anger:** Internalized rage that leads to self-harm, suicidal thoughts, negative self-talk, or chronic self-sabotage.

Unchecked anger can harm every aspect of a person's life. It strains relationships, hinders academic and professional growth, and disrupts sleep, spiking blood pressure, and damaging heart health. Frequent outbursts can alienate friends, coworkers, and even family members. Over time, this leads to a loss of trust, missed opportunities, and deteriorating self-worth.

The Psychology of Anger: Understanding the Role of the Primitive Brain

Anger is one of the most powerful and misunderstood emotions in the human experience. At its core, anger is not inherently bad—it's deeply wired into our biology as a protective mechanism. However, in the modern world, where threats are more psychological than physical, understanding how and why we get angry is crucial to managing it in healthier ways.

Anger and the Primitive Brain

Aggressive anger has deep roots in our evolutionary history. It originates in the most ancient part of our brain: the limbic system, particularly the amygdala—often referred to as the "primitive brain." This part of our brain evolved to keep us alive by responding rapidly to threats. When faced with danger, our ancestors had to fight, flee, or freeze. Aggressive anger was part of the fight response, a tool for survival in the face of physical threats (Richard, 2022).

This kind of anger served several vital functions in the animal kingdom:

- **Hunting:** Predators had to be fierce and aggressive to catch prey and survive.

- **Mating:** Competing for mates often required dominance and displays of power.

- **Territorial aggression:** Protecting one's environment from intruders was essential for safety and access to resources.

- **Parental aggression:** Parents needed a strong, often violent reaction to threats against their offspring.

- **Fear-induced aggression:** When an animal felt cornered or endangered, aggression served as a last resort to escape danger.

Humans share much of this instinctive wiring with animals. Though we rarely face threats from wild animals or rival tribes, our brains can still interpret modern stressors like criticism, disrespect, or rejection as threats to our safety or status. That's when the primitive brain takes over, and we respond with aggression.

The Spectrum of Anger: More Than Just Rage

Anger isn't a single emotion. It exists on a spectrum, from mild irritation to full-blown fury. According to Paul Ekman's *Atlas of Emotions* (2022), anger can manifest in various forms, each with its own psychological flavor and behavioral impact. Here are some of the key types:

- **Annoyance:** A low-intensity response to a minor inconvenience or irritation, like being cut off in traffic or interrupted during work.

- **Frustration:** Anger that arises when we are blocked from achieving a goal, such as dealing with slow technology or bureaucratic red tape.

- **Exasperation:** A stronger form of frustration, often directed at repetitive or persistent problems.

- **Argumentativeness:** A verbal expression of anger where one seeks to assert dominance or prove a point, often escalating conflict.

- **Bitterness:** A lingering, toxic form of anger that stems from feeling wronged or betrayed, often leading to ruminative thoughts.

- **Vengefulness:** A retaliatory form of anger that seeks to cause harm or inflict punishment in response to perceived injustice.

- **Fury:** The most intense form of anger—overwhelming, explosive, and often leading to physical or verbal aggression.

These emotions vary in intensity, duration, and consequence, but all of them share the common thread of threat perception, whether to our ego, goals, or sense of fairness.

Anger doesn't always roar. Sometimes it simmers. It can show up in less obvious forms, such as these (Richard, 2022):

- **Hostility:** The belief that others are out to get you. This often creates a defensive, suspicious stance toward the world.

- **Bitterness:** Replaying past wrongs in a loop, creating a chronic state of resentment and negativity.

- **Aggression:** When anger turns into action, often in a way that feels protective but ends up being harmful. This could be a lashing out in a heated moment or a preemptive strike in anticipation of conflict. People most commonly term aggression as "anger management problem," because this is the most visible form of anger.

While these responses may have served our ancestors well in the wild, they are often counterproductive in the context of modern relationships, workplaces, and society at large. What once protected us can now isolate us, damage reputations, and fuel cycles of conflict.

Key Takeaways

As we have seen, anger is a very normal human emotion, across cultures and periods, that can be rooted in a sense of injustice or self-preservation. Anger drove our ancestors to fight against threats. Social reform and quality improvements in human life are rooted in adaptive and justified anger. Instead of blaming the emotion, we need to address how we channel or react to anger. We should be cautious of maladaptive anger.

In the next chapter, we will explore in more detail the connection between ADHD and rage.

Self-Reflection

- What are the reasons you feel anger has become a problem for you? Check all that apply.

  - ☐ I feel "out of control."

  - ☐ It is affecting my relationships or career.

  - ☐ It always makes me feel guilty or ashamed later on.

  - ☐ I feel people treat me differently/ avoid me due to my anger outbursts.

  - ☐ I often get into trouble with authority because of my anger.

- Have you ever believed that your anger was the problem? If so, how did you try to "solve" the problem, and how did it work out for you?

- Have you ever used your anger as an excuse for your behaviour? What do you think needs to change about this attitude?

- What would you describe as your ideal reaction when angry? How would your life be different if you were able to behave like this going forward?

- Are you convinced that you are a) ready, b) willing, and c) able to change patterns of behavior around expressing your anger?

Chapter 2

ADHD and Impulsivity—How the Brain Amplifies Anger

Alex is an intelligent and well-spoken second-year university student currently sharing an off-campus apartment with two close friends. Over the past two summers, Alex worked as a camp counselor and described strong, positive relationships with both his fellow staff and the campers. Recently, however, he has been experiencing anger outbursts in his relationship with his girlfriend of one year. Although they share many common interests, he finds himself becoming irritable and lashing out when he feels overwhelmed or frustrated.

Alex is struggling with motivation and is dissatisfied with his recent academic performance. Despite being intellectually capable and imaginative, he feels he's not living up to his potential. The previous semester, he was placed on academic probation, which was a major turning point and led him to seek help with his inability to focus on academics. He feels that when under intense pressure, he tends to shut down emotionally and mentally, which contributed to his poor exam performance.

He has had behavioral and emotional challenges since his early high school years. Alex reports persistent difficulty with focus, time management, and a racing, restless mind. He frequently drifts off during lectures and has trouble staying engaged. When angry or frustrated, he often becomes defensive, snappy, and occasionally destructive. He's broken things or argued bitterly with his girlfriend during emotional flare-ups.

Alex admits to daily marijuana use, which he says helps soothe his constantly active thoughts and brings a sense of calm. While he's made efforts to reduce substance use, he's picked up smoking cigarettes—about half a pack per day—and is concerned that he's started to substitute marijuana with alcohol. Episodes of binge drinking with friends have also become more frequent.

His parents are increasingly worried. They recall how well he performed academically and socially in high school while still living at home, and they're troubled by the recent shift in his behavior and performance since moving away.

What Is ADHD? A Brief Overview of Attention Deficit Hyperactivity Disorder

Attention deficit hyperactivity disorder (ADHD) is one of the most commonly diagnosed neurodevelopmental conditions, marked by patterns of inattention, hyperactivity, and impulsivity. Despite growing awareness and understanding today, ADHD has a long and complex history that reflects evolving perspectives in psychology, medicine, and education.

A Historical Perspective

The first clinical description of ADHD-like behavior can be traced back to 1902, when British physician George Frederic Still presented a series of lectures describing children with difficulty sustaining attention and controlling impulses. He referred to it as a "defect of moral control," speculating that the cause might lie in brain dysfunction (Lange et al., 2010). Over the next several decades, the terminology changed frequently, highlighting how little was initially understood about the condition. Terms such as *postencephalitic behavior disorder*, *minimal brain damage syndrome*, *minimal brain dysfunction*, and *hyperkinetic impulse disorder* all reflected shifting theories of origin and symptomology.

Today, ADHD is recognized as a form of neurodivergence—a concept that encompasses natural variations in the human brain that result in different cognitive styles and behavioral patterns. Rather than viewing ADHD as simply a disorder or deficit, many experts now frame it as a different way of processing information and interacting with the world, though it may still involve significant functional challenges.

Defining ADHD Today

Many adults with ADHD experience difficulties in school, struggles in the workplace, or tension in personal relationships. They often face challenges with organization, job stability, meeting deadlines, managing daily responsibilities, and following through on long-term goals. A tendency toward restlessness may lead them to juggle multiple tasks simultaneously or act on impulse, sometimes taking risks without fully thinking them through.

Clinically, ADHD is a developmental condition that typically presents in one or more of the following forms (NIMH, 2021):

- **Inattention:** Difficulty focusing, staying on task, following through with responsibilities, and maintaining organization.

- **Hyperactivity:** Constant movement, fidgeting, or talking, often at inappropriate times.

- **Impulsivity:** Interrupting conversations, acting without thinking, or being unable to wait for one's turn.

Based on symptoms, a person can manifest one of three types of ADHD: inattentive ADHD, hyperactive-impulsive ADHD, or combined ADHD. ADHD may also present itself in a spectrum of mild to severe symptoms. Generally, these symptoms must persist over time, appear before the age of 12, and interfere with functioning across multiple settings—such as home, school, or work—to meet the diagnostic criteria.

Who Gets Diagnosed?

Historically speaking, ADHD was most commonly diagnosed in school-aged children, especially boys who exhibited disruptive hyperactive behaviors. For many years, it was assumed that children would eventually "outgrow" the condition. However, research now shows that ADHD can persist into adulthood, with symptoms evolving in form, rather than disappearing.

Current estimates suggest that ADHD affects approximately 5–7.2% of youth worldwide and around 2.5–6.7% of adults (Abdelnour et al., 2022), though many adults remain undiagnosed. It is also increasingly recognized that gender and cultural differences influence both the expression and detection of symptoms. For instance, girls may be underdiagnosed due to presenting with more internalized symptoms like daydreaming or anxiety, rather than the overt hyperactivity more commonly observed in boys.

Challenges in Diagnosis

One of the complexities of ADHD is that it lacks a single, definitive diagnostic test. Unlike physical conditions that can be detected with blood work, body scans, or imaging, ADHD must be diagnosed using a combination of clinical interviews, behavioral observations, and standardized assessment tools. A trained clinician evaluates a person's developmental history, symptoms, and functioning across settings to determine whether ADHD is present.

This process can be lengthy and is often influenced by social and cultural perceptions of behavior. In some regions, ADHD may be overdiagnosed, while in others, particularly where mental health resources are limited, it may be significantly underrecognized.

What Causes ADHD?

The precise cause of ADHD remains unknown, but a combination of genetic, biological, and environmental factors is believed to contribute. Family and twin studies have shown that ADHD has a strong hereditary component (Magnus et al., 2023), with genes involved in dopamine regulation playing a significant role.

Other factors linked to increased risk include (Yusuf Ali et al., 2022):

- **Prenatal influences:** Exposure to tobacco, alcohol, or environmental toxins during pregnancy.

- **Birth complications:** Low birth weight or premature birth.

- **Early environmental stressors:** Trauma, neglect, or chronic stress in early childhood.

It is important to understand that ADHD is not caused by poor parenting, excessive screen time, or sugar intake, though these may influence the severity of symptoms in some individuals.

ADHD Support

As understanding of ADHD continues to grow, so does the emphasis on individualized support and neurodiversity acceptance. While the condition can pose serious challenges in academic, occupational, and social settings, many people with ADHD also possess unique strengths, such as creativity, adaptability, and dynamic problem-solving.

The treatment for ADHD often involves a combination of approaches, including behavioral therapy, medication, coaching, and accommodations at school or work. A growing number of adults are now seeking late diagnoses, often after recognizing lifelong patterns of distraction, impulsivity, or emotional dysregulation that went unexplained.

Ultimately, ADHD is not simply a childhood disorder, nor is it a general condition with similar symptoms. It is a multifaceted neurological difference that calls for greater awareness, compassion, and support across the person's lifespan.

The ADHD Brain and Executive Functioning

ADHD is often characterized by difficulties with attention, hyperactivity, and impulsivity. However, beneath these observable behaviors lies a deeper, more complex issue—impaired executive functioning. Executive functioning refers to a set of cognitive processes that serve as the brain's "command center," enabling individuals to plan, prioritize, organize, manage time, regulate emotions, and respond adaptively to changing situations. These abilities are essential for navigating everyday life, and in individuals with ADHD, their disruption can lead to significant challenges.

Executive Functioning: The Brain's Command Center

Executive functions are largely governed by the frontal lobe, particularly the prefrontal cortex, which is responsible for higher-order thinking and self-regulation. Key aspects of executive functioning include (Diamond, 2013):

- **Working memory:** The ability to hold and manipulate information in one's mind over short periods.

- **Cognitive flexibility:** The capacity to shift thinking and adapt to new rules or perspectives.

- **Inhibitory control:** The ability to suppress impulses and resist distractions.

In people with ADHD, these functions often do not develop in sync with chronological age, leading to difficulties in self-management. This can manifest as disorganization, forgetfulness, difficulty completing tasks, or emotional overreaction. While these behaviors may appear to be due to a lack of effort or care, they are often the result of neurological differences that affect how the brain processes information and controls responses.

ADHD and the Impulsivity-Control Connection

One of the most prominent features of ADHD is impulsivity, or the tendency to act without sufficient thought or consideration of the consequences. This may go beyond interrupting conversations or blurting out answers; it can lead to self-sabotaging behaviors and long-term problems. People with ADHD may fully understand that certain behaviors, like binge eating, smoking, risky sexual behavior, or excessive spending, can have negative consequences, but they struggle to resist the urge in the moment.

This pattern is part of what we refer to as the impulsivity cycle (Richard, 2022). A stressor or emotional trigger, such as frustration, boredom, or anxiety, activates a strong urge. Acting on that urge brings temporary relief or gratification, which is soon replaced by feelings of guilt, shame, or regret. Despite promising themselves they won't repeat the behavior, the next trigger often revives the cycle.

This pattern can have serious implications, like broken relationships, professional setbacks, financial instability, and a sense of failure or worthlessness. The emotional toll can be especially heavy, as individuals may internalize these failures, further impairing their self-esteem and mental health.

Emotional Dysregulation in ADHD

ADHD isn't just difficulty paying attention or sitting still; it's also closely tied to emotional dysregulation, a challenge in managing emotional responses. Numerous studies have identified a link between ADHD and heightened impulsivity in three domains: motor (acting without thinking), cognitive (jumping to conclusions), and attentional (easily distracted or emotionally reactive) (Malloy-Diniz et al., 2024).

Individuals with ADHD are often more sensitive to emotional stimuli and less able to filter or delay their responses. As a result, they might react to minor frustrations with disproportionate intensity, struggle to calm down once upset, or swing rapidly from one mood to another. These emotional fluctuations can strain personal and professional relationships and complicate the process of self-reflection and growth.

Emotional dysregulation is not exclusive to ADHD, but is significantly more common among those with the condition. It can interfere with problem-solving, increase conflicts in relationships, and even mimic symptoms of mood disorders, making accurate diagnosis and treatment planning more complex.

The Impulsivity-Anger Link in ADHD

Anger, often viewed as a secondary emotion, typically stems from underlying feelings such as fear, pain, frustration, or helplessness (Ilagan, 2024). In ADHD, difficulties in self-regulation make individuals more vulnerable to these triggers and less capable of managing the resulting anger.

This can manifest as irritability, low frustration tolerance, or explosive outbursts, which may seem disproportionate to the situation. Since people with ADHD struggle to inhibit their initial emotional responses, anger can emerge quickly and with intense force. This contributes to a feedback loop—i.e., poor emotional regulation leads to outbursts, which cause interpersonal conflict or personal guilt, which in turn increases stress, feeding further dysregulation.

Understanding that anger is often a symptom rather than the core problem is essential for individuals with ADHD and those around them. Managing ADHD-related anger involves not just controlling outbursts, but also addressing the triggers and improving emotional self-awareness.

Developmental and Social Influences on Anger

Beyond ADHD itself, several developmental and environmental factors influence how individuals understand and express anger. For example:

- **Gender** (Suman, 2016) and **class socialization** (Park et al., 2013) affect whether someone is more likely to internalize (turn inward) or externalize (lash out) anger.

- **Parental modeling** (Plickert & Pals, 2019) plays a major role, as children often mimic how their caregivers express or suppress anger.

- The **manner in which caregivers respond to a child's strong emotions** (Sorin, 20023) can shape how safe they feel expressing strong emotions.

- **Peer interactions** and **social consequences** during adolescence can influence how individuals refine or hide their emotional and anger expressions over time (Shayanfar, 2016).

For individuals with ADHD, these factors interact with biological vulnerabilities to create a unique emotional landscape. Understanding these layers can lead to more effective support strategies, going beyond behavior control and focusing on emotional literacy, resilience, and self-compassion. Many people report specific "turning points" where they recognized that their way of handling anger needed to change, perhaps due to a lost friendship, job, or personal crisis.

Moving Toward Better Support and Understanding

Recognizing that ADHD affects far more than attention span is crucial for developing effective interventions. Treatments that target executive functioning, such as cognitive-behavioral therapy (CBT), ADHD coaching, time management tools, and mindfulness practices, can help improve planning, organization, and self-control. Medication, especially stimulants like methylphenidate and amphetamines, can also improve executive function by enhancing dopamine transmission in key areas of the brain.

However, most importantly, addressing emotional and behavioral symptoms such as impulsivity and anger should be part of a comprehensive treatment plan. This includes psychoeducation, support groups, and structured strategies for managing stress and emotional triggers.

Living with ADHD means managing a brain that processes the world differently, but it also means learning how to channel one's unique strengths. Many individuals with ADHD are highly creative, energetic, and passionate when given the right environment and with the right support. Executive functioning challenges can be daunting, but they are not insurmountable. With the right understanding, tools, and compassion, it's possible to break the cycles of impulsivity and emotional turmoil and move toward a more balanced, empowered life.

Key Takeaways

ADHD is not a "new" discovery. In fact, it has existed from time immemorial under various names and possibly for many, undiagnosed. It is no longer considered a mental health "problem." Today, we tend to view ADHD as a neuroatypicality, or rather, a different way in which the human brain processes knowledge and experiences. Our aim is not to "cure" ADHD, but to understand its core symptoms and workings so that people who fall under the spectrum can live fuller and more fulfilling lives.

In the next chapter, we are going to explore the ADHD cycle in more detail.

Self-Reflection

Impulsivity: Understanding Urges and Reactions

These questions help uncover what drives impulsive behavior and how it affects your life.

- What kinds of situations tend to trigger impulsive decisions or actions for me?

- When I act on impulse, what am I usually trying to avoid or escape (e.g., boredom, discomfort, stress)?

- Do I often regret my impulsive actions afterward? If so, what feelings usually follow—shame, guilt, relief, indifference?

- Have I noticed patterns in the types of impulsive behaviors I engage in (e.g., overspending, arguing, overeating, interrupting)?

- How do I justify my impulsive actions in the moment, and how do I feel about them afterward?

- What are the long-term consequences I've experienced as a result of impulsive behavior—on relationships, health, work, or self-esteem?

- Have I ever successfully resisted an impulse? If so, what helped me pause or reflect before acting?

Attention and Focus: Recognizing Distractions

These questions invite you to explore how attention issues show up in your daily life and thinking patterns.

- What kinds of tasks or environments make it hardest for me to concentrate?

- Are there specific times of day when my attention feels sharper or more scattered?

- Do I frequently jump from one task or thought to another without completing anything?

- How often do I lose track of what I'm doing mid-task, and what typically distracts me (internal thoughts or external events)?

- Do I find it hard to follow long conversations, movies, or written material without zoning out?

- When I try to focus, what thoughts or feelings interrupt my ability to stay on task?

- What strategies, if any, have helped me improve or regain focus when I feel scattered?

Hyperactivity and Restlessness: Understanding the Need to Move

These questions aim to explore physical restlessness and the mental sensation of "never slowing down."

- Do I often feel like I'm on the go or driven by a motor, even when I want to relax?

- In what ways do I express restlessness—through movement, speech, fidgeting, or mental racing?

- Do people in my life ever comment on my energy levels, pacing, or need to constantly be doing something?

- How do I typically respond when I'm required to sit still or be quiet for long periods?

- Does physical activity help me regulate my emotions or thoughts, and if so, how?

- Is my restlessness more mental (racing thoughts) or physical (can't sit still), or a mix of both?

- Have I developed habits (e.g., walking, tapping, constant multitasking) that help me cope with hyperactivity—or do they sometimes worsen it?

Self-Awareness and Patterns Over Time

These reflection questions connect the dots across impulsivity, attention, and hyperactivity to help form a fuller self-picture.

- Looking back, when did I first notice these behaviors or struggles—in childhood, adolescence, or adulthood?

- Have these challenges gotten better, worse, or stayed the same over time?

- How have these tendencies affected my relationships, career, or sense of self-worth?

- What would change in my life if I could manage these traits more effectively?

- What self-talk or beliefs do I carry about my attention span, behavior, or emotional control? Are they helpful or harmful?

Chapter 3

The ADHD Anger Cycle— Identifying Triggers and Reactions

Maris is a 36-year-old mother, living in Toronto with her husband of 11 years and their children, a four-year-old daughter and a two-year-old son. After stepping away from her dietetics career to raise her first child, she recently returned to work but now finds herself under mounting pressure as she juggles parenting duties with the rigorous demands of her profession.

Throughout her life, Maris has battled chronic concentration challenges. In elementary school, teachers provided extra support. She even used noise-reducing earplugs to study, but never received a formal learning-disability diagnosis. These focus and time-management struggles have followed her into adulthood, complicating everything from budgeting to maintaining a healthy work–family balance.

To compensate, Maris often creates high-pressure deadlines to stay on task. While this strategy sometimes works, it also fuels bouts of anxiety and depression, erodes her self-confidence, and leaves her feeling guilty, especially when she fears her work obligations come at the expense of time with her children.

At the clinic, Maris worries that she's underperforming. Procrastination and disorganization have crept into her daily routine, and with the added responsibilities at home, she can't concentrate on her caseload the way she once did. She often feels irritable or annoyed throughout the day.

Though intelligent and articulate, she nevertheless feels overwhelmed, often shutting down under stress instead of reaching out for help. She jokes that she needs a "life GPS" to find her way—"I'm so scattered," she admits. On top of these pressures, her stepfather and their aging cat are both battling advanced cancer.

Maris has been on a stable dose of antidepressants prescribed by her psychiatrist for the past eight years. Although she shows no signs of hyperactivity, she finds it nearly impossible to stay focused long enough to complete reading even a short article.

ADHD and Emotion: The Emotional Feedback Loop

Although ADHD is often characterized by inattention, hyperactivity, and impulsivity, emotional dysregulation (Shaw et al., 2014)—sometimes the "hidden" core symptom—plays a critical role in many individuals' day-to-day experiences. Understanding how emotions and ADHD interact requires unpacking an "emotional feedback loop" in which underlying neurocognitive features of the disorder amplify, prolong, and complicate emotional responses.

ADHD Subtypes and Emotional Vulnerability

As we have mentioned before, ADHD presents in three primary subtypes:

1. **Predominantly hyperactive-impulsive** ("impulsive/restless")

1. **Predominantly inattentive**

2. **Combined presentation**

Research indicates that individuals with the combined presentation exhibit the highest levels of emotional symptoms, including heightened irritability, mood swings, and sensitivity to stressors (Hirsch et al., 2019). Those with purely inattentive or hyperactive-impulsive profiles may not uniformly struggle with emotional regulation. What is evident is that emotional dysregulation is neither universal nor uniform across the ADHD population.

"Big Emotions" and Intensity

When there is emotional dysregulation, feelings often arrive with disproportionate intensity. Neuroimaging studies suggest that ADHD-related differences exist in the prefrontal cortex region, basal ganglia, prefrontal structures, and the corpus callosum (Beheshti et al., 2020; Albajara Sáenz et al., 2018; Giedd, 2019). Though the studies are inconclusive, some psychologists feel that these differences point toward limbic hyperactivity, which could lead to an amplified neural response to emotional stimuli, resulting in "big emotions," either positive or negative, that can escalate into frustration, anxiety, or depressive symptoms.

Moreover, working memory impairments common in ADHD (Kofler et al., 2020) can interfere with the brain's ability to "tag" an emotion as transient. Without sufficient working memory capacity to contextualize and moderate a feeling, a fleeting irritation or disappointment may become magnified, flooding the mind and body with unmitigated anger or distress.

The Feedback Loop in Action

To understand the working of the feedback loop, we can look at the following steps through which the mind of a person with ADHD might traverse (Brown, 2025):

- **Trigger:** A perceived slight or failure (e.g., missing a deadline) activates an emotional response.

- **Amplification:** Brain neural connectivity differences magnify feelings related to a trigger. (On the other extreme, there are also cases where an ADHD brain might fail to register, or seem insensitive to or unaware of other people's feelings.)

- **Flooding:** The individual feels overwhelmed by a singular, intense emotion like anger, shame, or anxiety.

- **Working memory breakdown:** Impaired ability to reframe or reevaluate the situation means the emotion persists and grows.

- **Behavioral outburst:** To relieve internal tension, the person may "act out" by yelling, throwing objects, or lashing out verbally or physically.

Manifestations of Dysregulation: From Overwhelm to Outburst

Emotional dysregulation in ADHD can take many forms, some of which include (Brown, 2025):

- **Emotional flooding:** Rapid onset of intense feelings, such as rage.

- **Rejection sensitivity:** Extreme hypersensitivity to perceived criticism or disapproval, known clinically as rejection sensitive dysphoria (RSD).

- **Emotional bottling:** Avoiding the expression of feelings due to fear of negative consequences, which paradoxically increases internal stress.

- **Denial/avoidance:** Refusal to acknowledge painful emotions, leading to dissociation or withdrawal.

- **Impulsive emotional carriage:** Being carried away by an emotion without pause for reflection.

When the feedback loop spirals unchecked, the individual may resort to dramatic expressions—screaming, throwing objects, or even physical aggression—to discharge the overwhelming emotional energy. These outbursts often produce immediate relief, reinforcing the cycle by teaching the brain that extreme expression "works" to alleviate distress, albeit temporarily.

The emotional feedback loop in ADHD is a neurobehavioral cycle wherein underlying regulatory deficits amplify and prolong emotional reactions. While not everyone with ADHD experiences these "big emotions," for those who do, the resulting dysregulation can severely impact relationships, work performance, and self-esteem. Effective interventions, such as cognitive-behavioral strategies, emotion-focused therapies, and, when appropriate, pharmacological support, work to strengthen prefrontal regulation, enhance working memory, and provide tools for recognizing and modulating intense emotional states before they trigger an outburst.

Identifying Triggers

When exploring anger in ADHD, it's crucial to distinguish between **state anger,** or short-lived bursts of intense irritation or rage, and **trait anger,** which is a more enduring tendency toward hostility. ADHD rage can be linked to either form of anger. However, there is a tendency for ADHD rage to be spiked by specific stimuli, too. In pinpointing the stimuli, or **triggers,** that excite these bursts of emotions, individuals can begin to anticipate, understand, and manage their emotional reactions.

Triggers can be people, places, events, or internal experiences that provoke feelings of discomfort like anger, frustration, anxiety, sadness, or fear. In ADHD, these triggers can rapidly escalate from a mild irritation to an overwhelming emotional flood, particularly when combined with the disorder's characteristic challenges in attention and executive function.

Why Identifying Triggers Matters

Tracking triggers is effective in managing your emotions before they build up and lead to a "blowup."

1. **Awareness:** Recognizing what sparks an emotional surge is the first step toward self-regulation.

2. **Control:** With awareness of the triggers, it becomes possible to choose responses rather than reacting impulsively.

3. **Empowerment:** Tracking triggers fosters a sense of agency because you're no longer at the mercy of unseen forces.

For some people, keeping an anger-trigger log can be an invaluable tool. In other words, each time you notice a state-anger spike, jot down details like:

- **what** happened (e.g., "Waiting on hold over call for tech support")

- **where** you were

- **who** was involved

- **how** you felt (physical sensations, thoughts)

- **what** you did in response

Over time, patterns will help you gain insight into why particular situations provoke anger. You can then develop tailored strategies to intercept the buildup.

Common ADHD-Related Triggers

While every trigger is unique for each individual, clinical experience highlights several frequent culprits in ADHD-related anger, such as the following:

- **Frustration and impatience:** Lines, on-hold phone calls, or slow drivers often spark a rapid anger surge.

- **Impulsive overreaction:** A fleeting thought like, "They ignored me," can become magnified into a full-blown rage.

- **Memory and attention lapses:** Forgetting an appointment or misplacing keys can feel catastrophic, fueling anger at oneself.

- **Social sensitivity:** Perceived criticism or rejection, even if unintended, can trigger intense hurt and anger.

- **Planning and deadline failures:** Missing a work deadline or forgetting to pay a bill often leads to self-blame and frustration.

- **Low self-esteem:** A persistent inner critic primes negative self-talk, making even minor setbacks feel devastating.

Context-Specific Coping Strategies

Because triggers and the underlying thought patterns they tap into are personal, coping methods must be personalized too. Below are some context-sensitive strategies to try in the moment:

- **Walk away for a cool-down:** If safe and feasible, leave the triggering environment. A brief pause, even five minutes, allows the physiological arousal to subside.

- **Validate your feelings:** Acknowledge your anger without judgment by saying, "I'm really mad right now, and that's understandable." Journaling or voice-memoing your thoughts can diffuse the charge.

- **Use an interim activity:** Say to yourself, "This will pass." Then engage in a soothing or distracting task like calling a friend, taking a brisk walk, or reading a few pages of a book, until the heat of the emotion dissipates.

- **Monitor early warning signs:** Catching anger before it peaks can prevent an outburst. Common early indicators include

- muscle tension in the neck and/or shoulders.

- jaw or fist clenching.

- flushed skin or sweating.

- increased heart rate or rapid breathing.

- a sudden "rush" of energy.

- shallow and rapid breathing.

- feeling hot or sweaty.

Environmental and Lifestyle Triggers

Sometimes, external factors subtly prime the emotional system for overload. Reducing these background stressors may also lower overall reactivity:

- **Auditory distractions:** Chatter, traffic noise, or a buzzing phone can erode patience. Consider using noise-cancelling headphones or a quieter workspace.

- **Visual clutter:** A messy desk or too many open browser tabs can heighten stress. Schedule regular "declutter" breaks.

- **Harsh lighting and strong odors:** If flickering fluorescents or pungent smells are irritating, soft lamps and air purifiers may help.

- **Overcrowding:** Busy malls or packed public transit can feel suffocating. So, plan errands during off-peak hours.

- **Sleep deprivation:** Even one night of poor rest amplifies irritability. Prioritize consistent sleep hygiene.

- **Unhealthy diet and inactivity:** Blood-sugar crashes and sedentary habits fuel mood swings. Balanced meals and regular exercise can support emotional stability.

- **Chronic stress:** Job pressures, academic deadlines, or caregiving demands accumulate stress. Build in restorative self-care routines to combat this.

Identifying and cataloging triggers is not an endpoint but rather a springboard to deeper self-understanding and resilience. It should also be remembered that since ADHD is closely tied with neural differences in remembering and processing information, the above steps or techniques may not be useful for everyone. Some may find it hard to recall or practice the techniques despite knowing them when in the heat of their emotions.

Hence, in later chapters, especially Chapter 9, we will explore more about cognitive behavioral therapy (CBT) and dialectical behavior therapy (DBT), which can help train the mind. CBT, in particular, is a valuable asset in improving the core symptoms of ADHD (Lopez et al., 2018). As part of the therapies, one can learn structured techniques for reframing trigger responses, strengthening emotional regulation skills, and integrating medication when indicated.

Remember, you can empower yourself to interrupt the cycle, learn, and choose more adaptive reactions, and transform moments of overwhelm into opportunities for growth by shining a light on the triggers that fuel ADHD and impulsive rage.

Breaking the Cycle: Reaction vs Reflection

A hallmark of ADHD-related impulsivity is acting first and thinking later, which can lead to regrettable outbursts and strained relationships. Learning to "slow down," or create a pause between impulse and action, allows time to consider consequences, regulate the flood of emotion, and choose a more constructive response.

Anger management is not only about managing emotions in the heat of the moment, but trying to create an environment where we manage other factors that place us at risk of overreacting. For example, if you want to squeeze in an extra activity into an already full day when your time is already limited, it could most likely lead to increased stress. You will be rushing, not paying attention to what is going on, maybe not listening to someone as they are trying to explain something to you. Your mind is busy thinking about how to get somewhere on time or do something, and the person speaking to you might get upset. In turn, you feel criticized and judged. Feeling defensive, and without enough forethought, you might respond in a way you don't intend to.

One of the best ways to minimize falling prey to a situation like the above would be to schedule activities and events well in advance and to stop trying to "maximize" your days. We make our lives harder by trying to be more effective or efficient. Instead, we need to monitor and decide what to drop to reduce unnecessary stress. This is an important strategy to help manage your daily flow, allowing you space to reflect and think. In this process, even if there are some setbacks, they will not be as stressful.

Start by thinking about all the factors that you can manage in advance. These may include, but not be limited to, things such as: poor relationships with people, your living conditions, and lack of self-care. Now think about how you can "slow down" in the long term.

Why Slowing Down Matters

When you are rushing toward an unknown or scary territory, wouldn't your first wish be to slow down a bit? Slowing down can help in the following ways:

- **Consequence evaluation:** Pausing gives you space to ask, "Will I regret this? Could I harm someone irreparably? Might this damage my career or relationships?"

- **Emotional cooling:** A brake on the situation reduces physiological arousal like heart rate, muscle tension, and adrenaline, so that intense anger or anxiety doesn't hijack your decision-making.

- **Shift from state to reflection:** Instead of a reactive burst of emotion ("state anger"), you can create room for thoughtful consideration ("reflective response").

One effective strategy we recommend in the anger management course on Impulsivity.com is the next exercise, which you can try out.

The "Stop-Think-Act-Recover" Framework

1. **Stop:** Physically or mentally hit the brakes as soon as you notice rising tension.

2. **Think:** Briefly play the tape all the way through, or imagine potential outcomes, both positive and negative, of expressing rage versus responding calmly.

3. **Act:** Choose a deescalating response. You can use one of the strategies in the list provided in the next section.

4. **Recover:** Reflect on what worked or didn't and integrate those lessons into future reactions.

Concrete Steps to Slow Down The Intensity of the Emotion

1. **Deep breathing and relaxing the body**

   - Engage in focused breathwork. Triangle breathing, which is inhaling for four counts, holding for four counts, and exhaling for six counts, can dampen the sudden rush of energy. Longer exhales in particular can be effective in slowing down the fight-or-flight response (Saline, 2024).

   - Consciously release muscle tension by rolling your shoulders, unclenching your jaw, and softening your grip.

2. **Pause or take a break**

   - If possible, step away from the triggering situation. For instance, excuse yourself to the restroom, go for a short walk, or simply turn your chair. Even a one-minute break can interrupt the emotional build-up.

- Use a mental time-out. Count silently to 10 or visualize a stop sign until you feel yourself calming down.

3. **Think outside the box**

   - ADHD brains often thrive on novelty and creativity. Use this to your advantage by reframing the situation. Ask yourself, "How might I view this from a different angle?"

   - Research shows that adults with ADHD often feel empowered by creative problem-solving, which can shift the focus from emotional reactivity to constructive innovation (Wadley, 2018).

4. **Timed distractions**

   - Listen to some music, read a page from a book, or play a game on your phone until you feel calmer and more in control of yourself.

Breaking the impulsive cycle in ADHD is less about eradicating anger and more about cultivating a habit of reflection. In time, with practice, you can strengthen neural pathways for emotional regulation. This deliberate "slowing down" will become an instinctive brake, transforming bursts of rage into opportunities for mindful choice and growth.

Key Takeaways

Filling your life with an endless number of activities or pursuits that will purportedly make you feel more productive may not help. Instead, learning to identify your personal triggers and developing strategies to cope with them is important in the long term. Similarly, living with ADHD also entails learning to slow down, plan, and pause before rushing into tasks.

In the next chapter, we'll explore brain chemistry in the light of ADHD rage in more depth.

Self-Reflection

Use the prompts below to reinforce the shift from reaction to reflection:

- **Trigger awareness:** What early signs signal that you are about to react impulsively?

- **Breathing audit:** Is there a breathwork technique that works best for you, and how long must you practice it to feel calm?

- **Creative reframe:** How else could you interpret this situation? What's a novel solution you haven't tried?

- **Consequence mapping:** What are three possible outcomes of reacting angrily? What are three possible outcomes of responding thoughtfully?

- **Recovery review:** After each incident, what did you learn about your triggers and "braking" strategies? What can you do differently next time?

Chapter 4

The Role of Neurotransmitters— Dopamine and the ADHD Response to Stress

Sarah sat at her kitchen table, her laptop open but blank, fingers drumming an erratic tattoo against the wood. She briefly looked at the stacks of unpaid bills and half-finished to-do lists she'd abandoned days ago. She'd promised her partner, Marcus, she'd sort them out by Sunday, today, but instead, she'd spiraled again, unable to focus, her mind ping-ponging between memories, worries, and half-formed ideas.

When Marcus walked in with two mugs of tea, hoping to share a moment of calm, Sarah snapped. "Why do you always think tea will fix everything?" she barked, yanking her mug from the counter until it teetered and crashed to the floor. Hot liquid splashed across the tiles. Marcus jumped back. He'd seen the flicker of fury in her eyes before, and the sudden, combustible anger that seemed to come from nowhere.

"I'm sorry, I'm sorry," she stammered as she began kicking the porcelain shards of the mug under the fridge, out of sight.

The apology felt hollow even to herself. She stormed past him, humiliated, letting the door slam so hard the walls rattled.

Once alone on the back porch, Sarah pressed her face to the cold glass of the door, trying to catch her breath. Her heart pounded. She hated that she'd lost control and disappointed Marcus again. She hated how ADHD made the simplest tasks feel so difficult, and how the frustration built up until she just snapped.

Twenty minutes later, Marcus opened the door again. Sarah had rearranged herself on the couch, knees drawn in, shoulders hunched. He handed her a fresh mug of tea. She didn't speak; she just accepted the tea. Her fingers shook.

Sarah hated her rage and how ADHD made her feel helpless. But in that moment, ashamed and vulnerable, she also felt relieved that Marcus stayed. She understood she would have to learn new coping tools, but first, she had to forgive herself for today. And that was the hardest work of all.

The Chemistry of ADHD

The chemistry of ADHD is deeply intertwined with our body's stress-response mechanisms and the regulation of key neurotransmitters. In individuals with ADHD, dysregulation of these systems can heighten mood instability, irritability, and anger. On that note, let's explore how the stress-response system and neurotransmitter imbalances contribute to anger and emotional dysregulation in ADHD, and highlight structural brain differences that underlie these phenomena.

The Stress-Response System in Anger

When we experience anger, our bodies activate a primal survival mechanism, the hypothalamic–pituitary–adrenal (HPA) axis and the sympathetic nervous system. The following are some effects of these:

- **Hormone release**

  - **Cortisol, adrenaline** (epinephrine), and **noradrenaline** (norepinephrine) surge into the bloodstream (Vanta, 2024).

  - These hormones trigger the "fight-or-flight" response, preparing muscles for rapid action and sharpening sensory perception.

  - They activate the "stress" mechanism of our body.

- **Sympathetic activation** (also known as the "gas pedal" of the nervous system)

  - Heart rate and blood pressure increase.

  - Blood flow is redistributed from "nonessential" systems like digestion to skeletal muscles, to aid running.

  - Glucose is rapidly mobilized in the system for immediate energy.

The above phenomena are a continuation of our primitive survival instincts. In earlier times, this acute stress response would have allowed humans to fend off predators or flee from threats. However, today's stressors like work deadlines, interpersonal conflicts, or financial worries rarely require physical confrontation or escape, yet our bodies still react as if survival is at stake. When anger flares over a project setback or relationship conflict, the instinctive hormonal cascade can exacerbate emotional reactivity rather than resolve modern challenges constructively.

Dopamine and Norepinephrine: The Neurochemical Roots of Mood and Anger

Two key neurotransmitters, dopamine (Vanta, 2024) and norepinephrine, play central roles in attention, motivation, and emotional regulation. In ADHD, their signaling is often deficient:

- **Dopamine deficiency**

    - Known as the "feel-good" neurotransmitter, dopamine mediates reward, pleasure, and motivation.

    - In ADHD, dopamine transporters may be overactive, clearing dopamine from synapses too quickly, or presynaptic neurons may release less dopamine overall.

    - Lower baseline dopamine levels correlate with irritability, mood swings, and a reduced ability to experience gratification, making frustration harder to tolerate.

- **Norepinephrine imbalance**

    - Norepinephrine enhances alertness, focus, and stress response.

    - Dysregulated norepinephrine signaling in the prefrontal cortex undermines executive functions like planning, impulse control, and emotional regulation, amplifying reactivity to perceived threats or frustrations.

Structural Brain Differences in ADHD

Beyond neurochemistry, individuals with ADHD often exhibit subtle differences in brain structure and activity, particularly in areas governing emotion and attention. Some of these could be in the following areas:

- **The frontal cortex,** which regulates our behavior, attention, and emotions, could be reduced in volume, or cortical thinning (Makris et al., 2007) might impair impulse control and planning.

- **The limbic system,** which governs emotions and motivation, could be affected by alterations in the amygdala and hippocampus (Cronkleton, 2021), contributing to mood lability. Mood lability is rapid and exaggerated shifts in emotional states, characterized by intense and often inappropriate emotional expressions.

- **The basal ganglia,** responsible for motor learning and behavior regulation, is where structural and connectivity differences disrupt habit formation and focus.

- **The default mode network (DMN),** responsible for mind-wandering and self-referential thoughts, could be out of connection with those areas responsible for attention and cognitive control (Sudre et al., 2017) or hyperactive at inappropriate times, leading to distraction and inattention.

Brain imaging for differences in structure and volume is still in its nascent stage, and more studies will need to be done before these causes can be definitively linked to ADHD. There aren't any brain imaging scans yet that can diagnose ADHD (Posner, 2020).

For now, certain interventions for ADHD and related rage today are based on the above general findings. Now, let's briefly look at some coping strategies that are often advised for ADHD, drawing from the above scientific and medical research.

From Chemistry to Coping

Understanding the interplay between hormonal stress responses, neurotransmitter imbalances, and brain structure can inform targeted interventions:

1. **Medication**

   - **Stimulants** (e.g., methylphenidate, amphetamines) increase synaptic dopamine and norepinephrine, improving attention and reducing irritability.

   - **Non-stimulants** (e.g., atomoxetine) selectively boost norepinephrine in the prefrontal cortex, aiding emotional regulation.

2. **Behavioral strategies**

   - **Mindfulness and relaxation training** can downregulate HPA axis activity, lowering cortisol reactivity when anger arises.

   - **Cognitive-behavioral therapy (CBT) and dialectical behavioral therapy (DBT)** help in identifying anger triggers, reframing negative thoughts, and practicing adaptive coping responses.

3. **Lifestyle modifications**

   - **Regular exercise** enhances dopamine and norepinephrine availability, stabilizing mood and reducing baseline stress levels.

   - **Structured routines** and breaks during demanding tasks help mitigate DMN overactivity and maintain focus.

ADHD-related anger and emotional dysregulation emerge from an intricate web of stress hormones, neurotransmitter deficits, and structural brain differences. While the "fight-or-flight" response once protected our ancestors, in modern contexts, it often exacerbates interpersonal and occupational challenges. Individuals with ADHD can gain greater mastery over anger, foster healthier relationships, and enhance overall well-being, leveraging pharmacological treatments, behavioral therapies, and lifestyle adjustments that target these underlying mechanisms.

ADHD and Reward Sensitivity

ADHD is characterized not only by inattention and hyperactivity but also by pronounced alterations in reward sensitivity (Littman, 2025). The neural circuits that process reward and reinforcement in ADHD are fundamentally shaped by dopamine dynamics, leading to a pronounced drive for immediate gratification and a propensity for impulsive behaviors. Below, we explore the neurobiological underpinnings of these phenomena.

ADHD often comes with a strong need for immediate rewards and quick fixes. This boils down to how the ADHD brain handles dopamine, a key "feel-good" chemical. When dopamine levels are low, a state called hypo-dopaminergic, everyday pleasures don't feel rewarding enough (Littman, 2025). To make up for this shortfall, people with ADHD may seek out activities or substances that give a big dopamine boost, such as sugar binges, risky driving, or even drug use. These behaviors can temporarily relieve unpleasant feelings but often lead to a crash afterward, bringing on irritability or a low mood.

Genetic factors can play a huge role in ADHD (Faraone & Larsson, 2019). Variants in certain genes that regulate dopamine and other "reward genes" contribute to what researchers call reward deficiency syndrome (RDS) (Blum et al., 2008). People with RDS have a stronger drive to find anything that sparks dopamine release, like drugs, alcohol, or thrill-seeking activities, just to feel normal.

Another key feature of ADHD is impulsivity, or acting without thinking, or perhaps being unable to control themselves from indulging in an action, despite knowing the negative consequences of doing so. People with ADHD tend to devalue future rewards more steeply than others—a pattern known as temporal discounting (de Water et al., 2024). In ordinary terms, this means a small reward now feels more attractive than a larger reward later. For example, someone might choose a quick snack over waiting for a healthier meal, or make a spontaneous purchase rather than save money.

When an ADHD brain does get a big hit of dopamine, say from gambling, binge eating, or extreme sports, it can often overshoot. The sudden spike in dopamine can feel good for a moment, but it's often followed by a "crash," where levels drop below the already low baseline. This crash can trigger sudden irritability, depressed mood, or even aggressive feelings, creating a cycle of chasing highs and crashing into lows.

On the flip side, some people with ADHD are overly sensitive to everyday stimulation. Normal-level lights or background noises, like fluorescent bulbs or crowded spaces, can feel overwhelming. In these cases, the brain's salience network— areas such as the insula and anterior cingulate cortex— overreacts to ordinary sensory input, causing discomfort and distractibility. This hypersensitivity can lead to a person avoiding busy environments or social situations.

So, what can help? First, medications, prescribed by an expert, such as stimulants (e.g., methylphenidate), boost dopamine and norepinephrine levels, evening out the highs and lows. Non-stimulant options (e.g., atomoxetine) work more subtly by increasing norepinephrine in critical brain areas, which indirectly supports dopamine function.

Second, behavioral strategies can harness the ADHD brain's reward system. Techniques like contingency management set up small, immediate rewards to reinforce positive behaviors, helping retrain the brain to value long-term goals. Cognitive-behavioral therapy (CBT) teaches skills for delaying gratification and managing impulsive urges.

Third, simple lifestyle changes make a difference. Regular exercise naturally raises dopamine levels and supports brain health overall. Creating structured routines, with regular meal times, breaks, and quiet spaces, helps reduce sensory overload and keeps focus on track.

A critical takeaway from contemporary research is that ADHD is a neurodevelopmental divergence and not a moral failing or lapse in character. The hypo-dopaminergic and stress-response abnormalities that drive impulsivity, reward-seeking, and mood lability are rooted in brain chemistry and genetics. With evidence-based medication, targeted behavioral therapies, and supportive environmental adaptations, individuals with ADHD can harness their unique neural wiring to thrive. Recognizing ADHD as a medical condition deserving of understanding and treatment empowers patients, families, and clinicians to adopt resilience-building practices and dismantle stigma.

The Neurobiological Link Between ADHD and Aggression

Anger and aggression often co-occur with ADHD, but they're not inevitable. Learning about the neurobiological connections can help us understand why some people with ADHD are more prone to outbursts and how we can intervene early.

First, research shows that anger in ADHD is often a comorbidity, meaning it frequently accompanies core symptoms (Nigg, 2025). That said, it isn't a defining feature of every case. However, the severity of ADHD symptoms, like inattention, hyperactivity, and impulsivity, tends to correlate with how often and how intensely anger and aggression appear. In other words, individuals with more pronounced ADHD traits often face greater provocation and more frequent aggressive episodes.

Importantly, not everyone with ADHD will experience aggression. For many, the challenge lies in distractibility or restlessness rather than irritability. But among children and preadolescents with ADHD, impulsive aggression or sudden, unplanned acts of anger are especially common (Saylor & Amann, 2016). These aggressive behaviors are distinct from premeditated aggression; they arise in the heat of the moment, and are driven by diminished impulse control and heightened emotional reactivity.

When left unaddressed, impulsive aggression can escalate into antisocial behaviors and increase the risk of criminal involvement later in life. For example, youth who struggle to regulate anger may have more conflicts at school, engage in physical fights, or associate with peers who reinforce aggressive conduct. Over the years, these patterns can erode social support and academic opportunities, perpetuating a cycle of marginalization and behavioral problems.

The good news is that early intervention can reduce these risks. Medication, particularly stimulant treatments, not only improves attention and reduces impulsivity but also dampens aggression by stabilizing dopamine and norepinephrine pathways in the prefrontal cortex, which are areas critical for impulse control and emotional regulation. By enhancing the executive function, medication gives people a bigger window to pause before reacting, shifting them away from immediate, emotion-driven responses.

Alongside medication, several behavioral therapies (refer to Chapter 9) for emotion regulation, such as anger management training, coping skills for recognizing early signs of anger, using self-talk to defuse tension, and practicing nonviolent ways to express frustration, could help further.

In sum, while ADHD can heighten the likelihood of impulsive aggression, it doesn't doom anyone to a lifetime of anger problems. Individuals with ADHD can manage their emotions, reduce aggressive incidents, and set the foundation for positive social, academic, and professional outcomes by recognizing aggression early, combining evidence-based medication with targeted behavioral interventions, and providing supportive environments.

Key Takeaways

We focused here on the neurobiological implications of ADHD and how it impacts the reward system of our brains. This gives us a clue as to why we might feel "out of control" while expressing heightened emotions, including anger.

In the next chapter, we will explore emotional dysregulation in particular.

Self-Reflection

- **"Time-out" planning:** Create a short, individualized "time-out" plan to use at the first sign of anger:

    - **signal** (e.g., notice clenched jaw)

    - **exit** (step outside or to a quiet room)

    - **self-soothe** (listen to calming music, use a stress ball, sip water)

    - **reentry** (return when you feel at least 30% calmer and use an "I" statement to express your need: "I need a minute to breathe.")

- **Mindful movement breaks:** Use short, regular bursts of physical activity to regulate stress hormones and boost dopamine:

    - Do 2–3 minutes of jumping jacks, marching in place, or wall push-ups every hour.

- Walk outside and count your steps up to 100.

- Stretch your neck, shoulders, and back while taking deep, slow breaths.

Integrating these micro-breaks into your routine can prevent anger build-up.

- **Grounding with the 5-4-3-2-1 method**: A quick way to shift focus away from escalating anger, this "sensory anchor" helps break the cycle of rumination and physiological arousal. You can engage your senses by identifying

  - **five** things you can see.

  - **four** things you can touch.

  - **three** things you can hear.

  - **two** things you can smell.

  - **one** thing you can taste.

- **Preemptive routine building**: Structure your day to minimize common ADHD stressors:

  - Use alarms or timers to break large tasks into 15-minute sprints with built-in breaks.

  - Plan "buffer time" between appointments to avoid rushing.

  - Schedule brief relaxation or movement sessions before known stress points (e.g., before a difficult meeting or family time).

- **Putting it all together**

  - **Practice regularly** when you're calm, so the techniques become more accessible under stress.

- **Combine strategies:** For example, use a grounding exercise during a "time-out," followed by a movement break.

- **Seek support:** Working with a therapist or ADHD coach can help tailor these exercises to your unique triggers and strengths.

You can strengthen your ability to notice rising anger, interrupt the stress cycle, and choose responses aligned with your long-term goals instead of momentary impulses by consistently practicing the self-help exercises above. Over time, this can build resilience and reduce the frequency and intensity of ADHD-related rage.

Chapter 5

Why ADHD Anger Feels Different —Emotional Dysregulation Explained

Anger is a powerful emotion, and while it's often seen as negative, it actually serves an important purpose. It signals that something important to us feels threatened or violated. Understanding what triggers anger can help us manage it more effectively.

People are usually moved to anger in four key scenarios (Richard, 2022). First, when something they care deeply about is involved, like family, relationships, or work. Small issues can feel enormous here because we zoom in on the details, overgeneralize, and lose perspective. This is sometimes called making a "mountain out of a molehill."

Second, anger can stem from feelings of self-diminishment— when we feel insulted, disrespected, or devalued. This can lead to black-and-white thinking, or seeing situations as either right or wrong, good or bad, with no room for compromise or shared understanding. Personalizing others' actions (e.g., "they did this *to* me") can amplify this reaction.

Third, anger often arises from a sense of powerlessness. When we feel out of control, we may fall into unhelpful mental habits like "mind-reading," which is assuming we know what others think, or "fortune-telling," or predicting negative outcomes. These distortions make situations feel worse than they are.

Fourth, unrealistic expectations play a big role. When we hold rigid beliefs about how things *should* be—how others should act or how life should unfold—we set ourselves up for disappointment and frustration.

Secondary causes also fuel anger. Unhealed emotional wounds, such as childhood neglect or harsh parenting, can make people more sensitive to perceived threats. If you were taught anger was the only safe emotional outlet, you might lean on it heavily. Additionally, if you tend to interpret people's actions as intentionally hurtful, it's easy to feel perpetually wronged.

Recognizing these patterns is the first step to changing them and gaining better control over your emotional responses.

What Is Emotional Dysregulation? An Overview of ADHD's Emotional Challenges

Emotional dysregulation is a common but often overlooked part of ADHD (Soler-Gutiérrez et al., 2023). While attention difficulties and impulsivity are well-known symptoms, emotional challenges can be just as impactful on daily life and relationships. Emotional dysregulation refers to difficulty managing emotional responses in a way that feels balanced and appropriate to the situation.

People with ADHD may

- react with emotions that feel out of proportion to the event.

- struggle to calm down, even if they *know* they're overreacting.

- feel overwhelmed quickly by frustration, annoyance, or even excitement.

- experience frequent mood swings or emotional outbursts.

- find it hard to shift their focus away from a strong emotional state.

They aren't being dramatic or overly sensitive; it's just how their brain processes and regulates emotions.

The Brain Science Behind Emotional Dysregulation

We have looked at this briefly in the preceding chapter, but let's try to understand it better. Emotional dysregulation in ADHD stems largely from how the brain handles emotional stimuli, especially due to imbalances between two key areas:

- **The amygdala:** This is the brain's emotional alarm system. It detects potential threats and triggers emotional responses like fear, anger, or excitement. In people with ADHD, the amygdala can be underactive (Viering et al., 2021) or smaller (Nárai et la., 2023), sending out wrong or stronger than necessary emotional signals even for minor triggers.

- **The frontal cortex:** This area is in charge of reasoning, impulse control, and emotional regulation. It helps evaluate whether an emotional reaction is necessary or helpful. In ADHD, the frontal cortex tends to be underactive and smaller (Arnsten, 2009), making it harder to inhibit or modulate strong emotions.

This imbalance can make emotional reactions feel intense and hard to control.

What Emotional Dysregulation Might Look Like in ADHD

Emotional dysregulation is not linked to ADHD alone. In fact, early research suggests that neurotypicals can not just show emotional dysregulation, but that it also manifests differently than in those diagnosed with ADHD (Nakashita, 2025).

It is equally important to understand that emotional dysregulation need not always and necessarily be anger, irritation, or annoyance. It can show up in different ways depending on the person. Here are some common signs:

- **sudden anger or anxiety spikes**, often disproportionate to the situation

- **crying easily**, not just from sadness, but also from frustration or even happiness

- **getting "stuck" in a feeling**, unable to move on or refocus attention

- **frequent mood swings**, sometimes without a clear cause

- **low frustration tolerance**, leading to quick irritation or withdrawal

- **trouble recognizing others' emotions**, which can lead to miscommunication

- **difficulty calming down**, even when trying to self-soothe

- **overemphasis on the negative**, like focusing only on what went wrong

- **hyper-excitement**, where joy or anticipation feels overwhelming

It's important to note that these responses aren't intentional. They're the result of neurological wiring that makes emotional control more challenging. But with awareness and the right strategies, including mindfulness, therapy, medication, or lifestyle adjustments, emotional regulation can improve.

Understanding that emotional dysregulation is a *neurological* challenge, not a personal failing, is the first step in reducing the shame or guilt and building healthier coping mechanisms.

ADHD and Heightened Sensitivity to Stress

Living with ADHD means more than just grappling with attention challenges or impulsive behaviors. It also involves a heightened sensitivity to stress. For many, the combination of emotional dysregulation, sensory overload, and internal overstimulation makes everyday stressors feel overwhelming.

One of the reasons people with ADHD are more vulnerable to stress is due to how their brains and bodies respond to it. The symptoms of ADHD, particularly emotional dysregulation, create a feedback loop where the stress of a situation is felt more intensely, lowering the person's threshold for stress over time. Essentially, the more frequently a person feels overwhelmed, the more sensitive they become to stress in the future.

The Role of Cortisol and the Body's Stress Response

Cortisol, often called the "stress hormone," is released by the body in response to stress. It's part of the body's natural fight-or-flight system and is essential for managing short-term challenges. However, when stress is chronic or perceived too frequently, as it often is in ADHD, it can lead to a consistently high cortisol state, which negatively affects both mood and physical health. Continuous stress can even lead to inflammatory dysregulation in the body, which can impact the brain and feed right into and aggravate ADHD symptoms (Saccaro et al.,2021).

Interestingly, research shows that while adults with both inattentive and combined types of ADHD can exhibit a typical cortisol response when faced with stress, those with inattentive symptoms tend to maintain *higher cortisol levels* even after the stressor has passed (Corominas-Roso et al., 2015). This suggests that some individuals with ADHD may struggle to "come down" from stress, lingering in a heightened state long after the stressful event is over.

Regardless of the specific cortisol patterns, people with ADHD consistently report experiencing high levels of subjective stress. In other words, they *feel* more stressed even if their physiological response appears normal.

The Hidden Weight of Sensory Overload

Another factor contributing to stress in ADHD is sensory overload. This occurs when the brain receives more sensory input than it can effectively process, resulting in overwhelm. For individuals with ADHD, sensory processing differences can mean that seemingly normal experiences, like background noise or tight clothing, become intense stressors.

Common triggers include the following (Mae, 2023):

- **Touch:** Unexpected or inconsistent physical contact, such as spontaneous hugs, firm pats, or even certain fabric textures, can be uncomfortable or even distressing.

- **Texture:** Scratchy clothes, restrictive materials, or unexpected sensations like the texture of certain foods or the feeling of water can create overwhelm.

- **Smell:** Strong scents, even those considered pleasant by most (like perfumes or shampoo), can be overpowering for someone with heightened olfactory sensitivity.

- **Sight:** Flashing lights, bright environments, or visually cluttered spaces can contribute to a sense of chaos and stress.

- **Sound:** Loud or layered sounds—like multiple conversations, sirens, or high-pitched noises—are among the most common triggers. For some, auditory overwhelm can lead to shutdown or irritability.

- **Taste:** Intense spices, strong flavors, or extreme temperatures in food can also provoke sensory discomfort.

This sensory sensitivity compounds the stress response. When your environment is a constant source of stimulation, your brain is always "on," leaving little room to relax or decompress.

Understanding the connection between ADHD and stress sensitivity—both emotional and sensory—can help individuals identify triggers, create calming strategies, and develop coping tools. The goal isn't to avoid all stress, but to manage it in ways that support mental and physical well-being.

The Role of Impulsivity in Emotional Reactions

Impulsivity is one of the hallmark symptoms of ADHD, and while it's often associated with rash decisions or speaking out of turn, its influence runs deeper, especially when it comes to emotions. In people with ADHD, impulsivity doesn't just affect actions; it can trigger sudden, intense emotional reactions that feel overwhelming and difficult to control.

For many, emotional shifts can happen rapidly—going from excitement to anger, calm to anxiety, or motivation to despair in what feels like a blink. These aren't mood disorders, but a reflection of how the ADHD brain processes and regulates emotions in real time.

What Rapid Emotional Shifts Look Like

People with ADHD often describe their emotions as intense, fast-moving, and hard to contain. These emotional shifts might look like (Gupta, 2023)

- being thrilled about something one moment, then suddenly feeling sad, anxious, or angry the next. These shifts are often triggered by something small.

- experiencing bursts of hyperfocus, only to later struggle to maintain attention or feel mentally drained.

- riding waves of energy and fatigue throughout the day, making it hard to maintain a steady rhythm.

- feeling emotions so strongly that they take over, pushing rational thought aside.

- getting upset or irritated more often and more easily than others.

- struggling to remain calm or seated during moments of frustration or boredom.

These patterns can be exhausting—not only for the person experiencing them but also for those around them. It can feel like you're on an emotional roller coaster with no clear "off switch."

Impulsivity's Hidden Role

At the core of these emotional swings are impulsive reactions, the tendency to act or react without a pause. The brain's

Impulse and Fire

impulse control system, primarily located in the frontal cortex, is less active in ADHD. That means there's often little buffer time between feeling an emotion and expressing it. This can lead to

- interrupting others during conversations, not out of rudeness, but because the thought feels urgent to share.

- blurting out comments without realizing they might hurt someone's feelings, only to feel regret later.

- rushing through tasks, causing mistakes that feel frustrating and demotivating.

- saying or doing something in a moment of emotion, whether in excitement or anger, and then dealing with the consequences once the moment passes.

Many people with ADHD struggle to pause, reflect, and regulate before acting. That "pause" is where regulation happens for most people—but in ADHD, that moment is often missing.

The Good News: Understanding Leads to Change

While these challenges are real, they're also manageable. The first step is *awareness*—recognizing the role impulsivity plays in emotional shifts.

With practice and the right strategies, such as mindfulness, cognitive behavioral therapy (CBT), medication, and self-regulation techniques, people with ADHD can learn to slow down emotional reactions, recognize their triggers, and respond in more intentional ways. It doesn't mean they may stop feeling strong emotions, but gaining more control over how those emotions are expressed.

Again, impulsivity isn't a flaw; it's a trait that, when understood and channeled, can even be a strength. The key is learning to manage its impact, especially in emotional moments.

Emotional Flooding: How ADHD Can Lead to Intense, Unmanageable Emotions

One of the most overwhelming emotional experiences for people with ADHD is emotional flooding, a state where emotions become so intense that they feel unmanageable, chaotic, or even frightening (Brown, 2025). This is a neurological response where the brain is essentially overwhelmed by too much input, too quickly, without enough capacity to regulate it.

Emotional flooding occurs when strong emotions—like anger, fear, or anxiety—build up rapidly and flood the brain's ability to respond logically or calmly. It often feels like being hijacked by your own feelings, leaving you unable to think clearly, communicate effectively, or make safe decisions.

Common Signs of Emotional Flooding

During an episode of emotional flooding, the body may react intensely, both emotionally and physically. People with ADHD might experience the following (*Why are my feelings so intense?*, 2024):

- a **sudden, intense urge to hurt someone or something,** not out of malice but as a reaction to feeling cornered or out of control

- a powerful **impulse to lash out,** yell, or break something as a way to release emotional pressure

- a desperate **need to escape, hide, or disappear—** commonly misinterpreted as avoidance or defiance

Impulse and Fire

- feeling **frozen or paralyzed,** unable to move, think clearly, or articulate what's happening

- **increased heart rate, rapid breathing, sweating,** and **muscle tension**—classic signs of the body's fight-or-flight response

This state can last for minutes or hours and often leaves a person feeling exhausted, ashamed, or confused afterward. For someone with ADHD, this isn't a sign of weakness—it's a neurological overload.

Why ADHD Increases the Risk of Emotional Flooding

People with ADHD often live in a state of high emotional and sensory arousal. Because their brains struggle with regulation, even a small trigger can escalate quickly. Emotional flooding is more likely to occur when

- there's accumulated stress from the day.

- they feel misunderstood or invalidated.

- they're faced with overwhelming tasks or expectations.

- their sensory environment is too stimulating (e.g., loud noises, bright lights, crowded spaces).

The underlying neurology makes it harder for people with ADHD to "hit the brakes" once emotions start rising. Without that internal pause, emotions can erupt or implode before self-control kicks in.

The Long-Term Impact of Emotional Impairment

This difficulty with emotional regulation can have wide-reaching effects. Research shows that emotional dysregulation and flooding in ADHD are linked with the following (Soler-Gutiérrez et al., 2023):

- **higher accident rates**, due to impulsive or emotionally driven decisions

- **substance misuse**, often used as a way to numb or manage overwhelming emotions

- **mental health challenges**, such as anxiety, depression, or comorbid disorders like oppositional defiant disorder (ODD) or bipolar disorder

- **struggles in academic and professional settings**, where emotional outbursts or low frustration tolerance can hinder performance

- **strained personal relationships**, especially when emotions are misinterpreted or expressed in ways that hurt others

- **low self-esteem**, fueled by regret, guilt, and feeling "too much" or "not in control"

With self-awareness, professional support, and tools like emotional regulation strategies, mindfulness, and therapy, people with ADHD can begin to recognize early signs of flooding and learn how to intervene before emotions spiral.

Key Takeaways

We have looked at ADHD and its close connection with emotional dysregulation, emotional flooding, impulsivity, and a host of other emotional management problems.

In the next chapter, let's look in detail at the effect of emotions spiraling out of control in a person's professional and personal life.

Impulse and Fire

Self-Reflection

Understanding Your Rage

What does anger feel like in my body?

- (e.g., tight chest, clenched fists, fast heartbeat)

What typically triggers my rage?

- Are there patterns like being interrupted, feeling ignored, or sensory overload?

What do I usually think right before I lose my temper?

- (Look for thoughts like "They don't respect me" or "I can't take this anymore.")

How do I react when I'm angry?

- What words, actions, or behaviors do I notice?

What do I feel *after* an outburst?

- (Shame? Relief? Confusion? Regret?)

How was anger handled in my home growing up?

- Did you learn to suppress it, express it explosively, or were you punished for it?

Do I give myself permission to feel angry without judgment? Why or why not?

Self-Awareness Exercises: Calming the ADHD Rage Storm

- **Anger log:** Keep a daily or weekly log of situations that triggered anger. Include what happened, how you felt, what you did, and what you might do differently next time.

- **Reframe the thought:** Pick a common anger-triggering thought (e.g., "No one listens to me") and practice reframing it into something more balanced (e.g., "I feel unheard right now. I can express myself calmly.").

- **Compassion letter:** Write a letter to yourself from a kind, nonjudgmental perspective. Acknowledge how hard it is to deal with emotional flooding and how much strength it takes to work on it.

Chapter 6

The Impact of Untamed Anger— Relationships, Work, and Self-Esteem

Anger in individuals with ADHD often presents differently than in the general population. While everyone experiences anger, individuals with ADHD may experience it more intensely, more frequently, and with far less warning. This chapter explores the roots of that anger, its internal and external triggers, and the impact it can have on relationships.

As we have seen, anger does not appear in a vacuum. In individuals with ADHD, it can be triggered by internal experiences or external stimuli, often both. Understanding these triggers is a critical step in managing emotional reactivity and cultivating healthier relationships.

We also saw how triggers escalate ADHD emotional dysregulation. Internal triggers refer to emotional states or thoughts that arise from within the individual. People with ADHD often experience emotional dysregulation, impairing the ability to modulate feelings appropriately. As a result, seemingly minor emotions like disappointment, sadness, anxiety, or loneliness can rapidly escalate into anger. In many cases, anger acts as a defensive emotion, masking more vulnerable feelings that may be harder to express. For example, an individual who feels rejected or misunderstood may lash out in anger rather than admit to feeling hurt or insecure.

External triggers, on the other hand, involve sensory or environmental factors. Because individuals with ADHD often exhibit heightened sensitivity to sensory input, something as minor as a loud sound, a strong smell, or an unexpected touch can become overwhelming. Other common external triggers include reminders of past conflicts, feeling crowded or having one's personal space invaded, or encountering frustrating bureaucratic processes. These triggers can quickly lead to a state of emotional flooding, where the ability to regulate responses is compromised.

A defining feature of ADHD-related anger is low frustration tolerance—the inability to cope with even minor setbacks or challenges. This means that tasks requiring patience, delayed gratification, or long-term thinking can feel disproportionately difficult.

As a result, people with ADHD might explode in anger when faced with everyday challenges such as a traffic jam, a misplaced item, or a technological glitch.

ADHD and Interpersonal Struggles

Relationships, whether romantic, platonic, or familial, require emotional availability, attentiveness, and communication. Unfortunately, these are areas where individuals with ADHD may struggle profoundly, especially when anger is left unchecked.

Impulse and Fire

One of the most common issues is the lack of focus on others' emotional needs. This is not due to selfishness, but rather attentional dysregulation. A person with ADHD may intend to be present and supportive but can become distracted, forgetful, or overly focused on their own internal experience. Over time, this perceived inattentiveness can lead loved ones to feel ignored or unimportant.

The impulsive disorder that may accompany ADHD further complicates things. Words are often spoken before being thought through, and actions taken in the heat of the moment may hurt others unintentionally. An angry retort, a sarcastic remark, or a dismissive tone, delivered impulsively, can leave lasting wounds, even when quickly regretted.

At home, an ADHD executive dysfunction may make it hard to manage domestic responsibilities. Forgetting to pay bills, missing appointments, or failing to contribute equally to household tasks can breed resentment. These missteps are often interpreted by partners or family members as signs of laziness or lack of care when, in reality, they stem from cognitive challenges related to planning, memory, and organization.

Though we think of rage as equivalent to violence, at times, rage can also lead to inaction, passive aggression, and what may look like callousness. People who tend to bottle up rage can often respond with coldness by refusing to talk or engage with their partners or family members, escalating tension and stress in relationships.

The Cost of Rage: How Anger Affects Relationships

When anger is frequent and poorly regulated, it creates a toxic atmosphere that corrodes trust and intimacy. Over time, patterns of conflict, miscommunication, and emotional volatility become entrenched. These are some of the consequences commonly seen in relationships affected by ADHD rage:

- **Whirlwind romances that fizzle out:** People with ADHD may dive headfirst into new relationships, driven by emotional intensity and novelty-seeking. But as the relationship stabilizes and routine sets in, their interest may wane, or irritability may increase. Partners are often left feeling confused and whiplashed by the hot-and-cold behavior.

- **Misunderstandings and emotional disconnect:** Anger may be interpreted as hostility when it is actually frustration or overwhelm. Because communication tends to break down during outbursts, loved ones may begin to walk on eggshells, avoiding sensitive topics altogether.

- **Escalation to abusive dynamics:** In extreme cases, unmanaged ADHD-related anger can contribute to patterns of intimate partner violence, including verbal, emotional, physical, or even sexual abuse. While not all individuals with ADHD are abusive, untreated emotional dysregulation can dramatically increase the risk of crossing relational boundaries in harmful ways.

- **Family alienation:** Parents, siblings, and even children may distance themselves from someone whose anger feels unpredictable or disproportionate. Over time, emotional closeness gives way to guardedness and withdrawal.

Five Warning Signs of Relationship Damage Due to Anger

If you have ADHD and are experiencing difficulties in your personal relationships, it may be helpful to reflect on these five signs that anger is causing harm (Richard, 2022):

1. **People avoid conflict with you.** If others are hesitant to disagree or share negative feedback, it may be a sign that they fear your reaction.

2. **People change how they interact with you when you're angry.** Do loved ones grow quiet, tense, or defensive when you raise your voice or become agitated?

3. **Relationships have ended or changed after conflicts.** If friends, partners, or family members have distanced themselves after arguments, the way anger is expressed may need reexamination.

4. **People react negatively to you more often.** Consistent irritation, avoidance, or passive-aggression from others can indicate that they are responding to how you manage your emotions.

5. **You're surprised by how much something bothered them.** If others bring up emotional hurts that you don't remember or didn't recognize as significant, it suggests a disconnect between intention and impact.

Understanding the roots of ADHD rage and its effects on relationships is not about assigning blame; it's about building insight and fostering change. Emotional regulation is a skill that can be developed, and relationship repair is always possible when there is accountability, compassion, and a commitment to growth.

Apart from therapies like CBT and DBT, which have shown strong results in helping individuals with ADHD manage anger and impulse control, ADHD-specific coaching, medication management, and relationship counseling can play a crucial role in breaking cycles of reactivity and restoring connection.

While anger may be part of the ADHD experience, it doesn't have to define your relationships. With the right tools and support, you can cultivate emotional resilience, deepen your connections, and experience more peace within and around you.

Road Rage, Addictions, and Other Risky Behaviors

Unchecked ADHD-related anger doesn't just affect relationships—it can lead to impulsive and dangerous behaviors that put both the individual and others at risk. The same emotional dysregulation and impulsivity that cause outbursts in personal settings can play out behind the wheel, in addictive behaviors, or in self-directed harm.

Road Rage and Driving Risks

Individuals with ADHD often experience difficulty regulating frustration during high-stakes or high-pressure situations, such as driving. Road rage becomes a common expression of this dysregulation. Anger behind the wheel may lead to blaming other drivers for minor infractions, aggressive shouting, tailgating, and even physically dangerous behavior like intentionally cutting off or driving into others. Research has shown that individuals with ADHD are more prone to traffic violations and accidents, largely due to impulsivity, distractibility, and intense emotional reactions (Fuermaier et al., 2017).

These behaviors are not just emotionally driven—they are neurologically rooted. The prefrontal cortex, responsible for judgment and inhibition, often under-functions in ADHD brains, especially under stress. When anger flares in the car, rational thinking is often overridden by immediate emotional reactions.

Addictions and Self-Harm

When rage becomes chronic or overwhelming, some individuals turn to substances and behaviors to self-medicate.

Untreated impulsivity and emotional pain can lead to lifelong struggles with alcohol, drugs, nicotine, binge eating, gambling, or risky sexual behaviors. These addictions often begin as coping mechanisms to blunt intense emotions or provide momentary relief, but can evolve into serious dependencies that further harm emotional health and relationships.

Importantly, rage is not always turned outward—it can be directed inward. Research links ADHD, particularly when comorbid with depression, to higher risks of self-harm and suicide (Lin et al., 2024). Emotional intensity combined with impulsivity can create dangerous situations where someone acts on a momentary but overwhelming sense of pain, guilt, or worthlessness.

Recognizing these patterns is the first step toward safety and healing.

Workplace Friction: The Role of Anger in Professional Life and Career Progress

The symptoms of ADHD, particularly emotional dysregulation, impulsivity, and difficulties with focus, can pose unique challenges in the workplace. While people with ADHD often possess remarkable strengths, including creativity, passion, and the ability to hyperfocus, these traits can be overshadowed by the emotional friction that arises when anger is mismanaged. This tension can hinder career progress, damage professional relationships, and lead to long-term financial and psychological consequences.

Hyperfocus vs Emotional Dysregulation at Work

One of the paradoxical traits of ADHD is hyperfocus, an intense, sustained concentration on tasks of high interest. When channeled effectively, hyperfocus can make someone with ADHD an exceptional employee. They may thrive in project-based roles, creative industries, or in high-pressure environments that demand fast thinking and innovation. In fact, many individuals with ADHD excel in entrepreneurial settings, where their ability to pivot quickly and think outside the box becomes an asset.

However, this cognitive strength often comes at a cost. Hyperfocus can lead to the exclusion of social and emotional awareness. A person may become so engrossed in a task that they miss important social cues, skip meetings, ignore emails, or neglect collaborative efforts. These behaviors can come across as aloof, disrespectful, or uncooperative to peers, managers, and subordinates.

Furthermore, emotional interactions in the workplace are often difficult for individuals with ADHD. They may struggle with impulsive reactions to feedback, perceived criticism, or bureaucratic inefficiencies. Emotional outbursts, passive-aggressive communication, or withdrawal after a confrontation can alienate colleagues and create a reputation for being volatile or unprofessional.

Focus, Time Management, and Productivity

Not all people with ADHD experience hyperfocus. For many, the greater challenge lies in sustaining attention and managing time effectively. Studies have found that adults with ADHD had significantly poorer outcomes in employment, including higher rates of job loss, lower earnings, and more frequent workplace conflicts (Hotte-Meunier et al., 2024). Time blindness, difficulty prioritizing tasks, and forgetfulness often lead to missed deadlines, reduced productivity, and chronic underperformance.

In fact, one study found that adults with ADHD lost an average of 35 more workdays per year compared to their non-ADHD counterparts (Kessler et al., 2005). This reduced work output and reliability can jeopardize job security, limit opportunities for advancement, and create a cycle of employment instability.

Long-Term Impacts: Financial and Emotional Toll

The ripple effects of ADHD-related workplace struggles extend far beyond the office. Individuals with untreated or poorly managed ADHD are at increased risk of losing household income, often due to underemployment, frequent job changes, or periods of unemployment.

These financial setbacks are compounded by the psychological toll of repeated failure, job loss, or being misunderstood. Over time, workplace struggles can contribute to chronic stress, anxiety, depression, and burnout. Stress-induced physical illnesses such as high blood pressure, migraines, and gastrointestinal issues are also more common among adults with ADHD.

Stigma and Discrimination in the Workplace

In many professional environments, ADHD remains poorly understood. Employees may face stigmatization for their behaviors—being labeled lazy, careless, difficult, or emotionally unstable. A lack of awareness among employers and HR personnel often means reasonable accommodations are not provided, leaving individuals with ADHD without the support they need to succeed.

Fear of judgment can also discourage individuals from disclosing their diagnosis, preventing them from accessing potential workplace accommodations like flexible schedules, noise-cancelling tools, or task reminders. This leads to a hidden struggle, where the employee masks their symptoms while internalizing guilt and frustration.

Moving Toward Supportive Work Environments

Addressing workplace friction caused by ADHD-related anger and executive dysfunction starts with awareness, empathy, and practical support. Cognitive behavioral therapy (CBT), ADHD coaching, and workplace accommodations can dramatically improve both emotional regulation and job performance. Furthermore, educating managers and colleagues on the nature of ADHD can foster a more inclusive culture where neurodiverse individuals are empowered rather than penalized.

With the right strategies and support systems, individuals with ADHD are able to not only manage their anger more effectively but also thrive professionally—bringing their unique strengths to teams and organizations in meaningful, impactful ways.

The Self-Esteem Spiral: When ADHD and Anger Turn Inward

The emotional volatility of ADHD doesn't just damage relationships and careers; it can shape the way individuals view themselves. The self-esteem spiral is the painful loop many people with ADHD fall into—a cycle of anger, regret, negative self-perception, and emotional withdrawal. Left unchecked, this pattern can lead to deep-rooted shame, social isolation, and chronic emotional distress.

Anger and Negative Self-Perceptions

Anger is often thought of as an external behavior, but for individuals with ADHD, it can just as easily be internally directed. After an emotional outburst, many people with ADHD are consumed by guilt, embarrassment, and self-criticism. They might replay the interaction over and over, berating themselves for being "too much," "too reactive," or "broken." These negative evaluations can quickly evolve into deeply entrenched low self-esteem, especially if the episodes are frequent.

At the core of this spiral are cognitive distortions—irrational thought patterns that skew perception. Common distortions in ADHD include

Impulse and Fire

- catastrophizing ("This one mistake means I'm a failure.").

- black-and-white thinking ("Either I'm perfect or I'm worthless.").

- personalization ("They're upset—it must be because of me.").

- emotional reasoning ("I feel ashamed, so I must have done something wrong.").

These distorted thoughts become habitual, further entrenching feelings of self-loathing, hopelessness, and frustration. While a deeper exploration of cognitive distortions will follow in the next chapter, it's important to note how they reinforce both anger and a poor self-image, making it increasingly difficult to break the cycle.

Social Isolation and Shame

As anger goes unchecked and emotional wounds accumulate, social relationships suffer. Friends and family may pull away, confused or exhausted by unpredictable emotional outbursts. At the same time, individuals with ADHD may begin to isolate themselves, believing they're "too much" for others or convinced they always "mess things up."

Over time, this can result in

- chronic loneliness.

- a deepening sense of shame.

- avoidance of social situations.

- withdrawal from support systems.

Adding to this spiral are the feelings of being different— struggling to manage social cues, forgetting important dates, interrupting conversations, or feeling emotionally overwhelmed in group settings. People with ADHD often describe feeling like outsiders, constantly battling an internal sense of inadequacy and unpredictability.

Some of the core issues that fuel isolation and shame include

- poor working memory ("I forget what I'm supposed to say/do.").

- fluctuating emotions ("I'm never sure how I'm going to feel.").

- low self-esteem and self-worth ("Why would anyone want to be around me?").

- inconsistent performance ("Sometimes I do great, other times I can't even show up.").

These feelings can become so overwhelming that the person begins to give up on forming meaningful connections or achieving personal goals, reinforcing the cycle of failure and internalized anger.

Setting Realistic Expectations for Healing

For many, managing ADHD rage will be a lifelong journey, marked by periods of progress and setbacks. One common pattern is the cycle of overcommitment and emotional burnout. Many individuals start strong, overexcited and motivated, but soon crash due to the overwhelming energy demands or emotional fallout. This "boom and bust" cycle can worsen feelings of inadequacy.

The path to healing lies in radical acceptance, acknowledging both the challenges and the strengths of living with ADHD. This means

- accepting that not everyone will understand or support your struggles.

- recognizing that your symptoms are real, even if others minimize them.

- committing to personal responsibility while also asking for help when needed.

It's essential to strike a delicate balance between owning your emotional reactions and behaviors and setting boundaries around how others treat you. You are responsible for how you manage your anger, but that doesn't mean you must tolerate dismissiveness, gaslighting, or emotional neglect from others.

Self-compassion, therapy, peer support, and education can help break the self-esteem spiral. By understanding your neurobiology, building tools to regulate emotion, and reengaging with others in meaningful ways, it is possible to create a more stable, connected, and self-respecting life.

Key Takeaways

What is evident is that unmanageable bouts of rage can ruin personal relationships, performance at work, and even get a person enmeshed in unwanted legal tangles. All this can negatively affect one's mental health, self-perception, and self-worth.

In the next chapter, we shall examine the method by which ADHD and anger feed off each other and some ways to break this cyclical pattern.

Self-Reflection

- **ADHD strength + struggle mapping:** To build self-compassion by balancing challenges with capabilities,

  - draw two columns: "My ADHD Struggles" and "My ADHD Strengths."

  - fill in 5—7 items in each.

- Example struggles: "Impulsive reactions," "forgetfulness," "overwhelm in social settings."

- Example strengths: "Creative problem-solver," "hyperfocus on passions," "deep empathy."

This exercise counters low self-esteem by acknowledging the full spectrum of your ADHD traits, and not just the pain points.

- **Radical acceptance statement writing:** To promote emotional resilience and long-term acceptance,

  - reflect on what you're currently struggling to accept about yourself or your ADHD (e.g., repeated emotional outbursts, lost relationships, underperformance).

  - Write a short paragraph starting with, "Right now, I am learning to accept that..."

    - Include both the challenge and your intention to take responsibility.

    - Example: "Right now, I am learning to accept that I sometimes overreact when I feel rejected. I don't like this pattern, but I'm committed to understanding it and responding differently next time."

This exercise encourages self-compassion without denial, helping you move forward instead of getting stuck in guilt or denial.

Chapter 7

Breaking the Cycle—How ADHD and Anger Feed Each Other

Melissa is a 39-year-old accountant who was diagnosed with ADHD two years ago after a lifetime of feeling "off" but never knowing why. Though she excels at analytical tasks, her emotional regulation is a constant struggle, particularly explosive anger that flares up during high-stress periods, like tax season or when she's under pressure from clients or supervisors. One misplaced spreadsheet formula or critical email can ignite a disproportionate rage that blinds her judgment and leaves her emotionally wrecked.

But the rage is just the start. What truly eats at her is what follows—the shame, hopelessness, and brutal self-talk. Melissa spirals into cognitive distortions like black-and-white thinking that tell her, "I can't even control myself, I shouldn't be in this job"; overgeneralization, which makes her tell herself, "I always screw things up"; or emotional reasoning such as, "I feel like a failure, so I must be one." These thoughts chip away at her self-confidence, making it impossible to believe that change is within reach.

She tries several coping mechanisms like breathing exercises, journaling, and Post-it notes with affirmations, but in moments of stress, they feel childish or ineffective. Her ADHD makes follow-through inconsistent, and every slip reinforces the belief that she's irreparably flawed. She imagines coworkers rolling their eyes, secretly thinking she's unstable. Medication offers some stability, but it doesn't silence the constant voice that reminds her she's broken beyond fixing.

Melissa wants to break the cycle. She reads books on ADHD, attends therapy, and even considers support groups. But when things don't improve quickly, she feels crushed and convinced that this must mean she's incapable of growth. The hardest part isn't even the rage anymore. It's believing, deep down, that maybe there *is* something wrong with her. That belief is what most holds her hostage.

Understanding the Vicious Cycle: How Anger Increases Impulsivity and Vice Versa

Melissa's rage doesn't appear out of nowhere. It builds like pressure in a fault line. The more she tries to suppress it, the more it demands release. And when it erupts, it often feels like she's watching herself from outside her body, unable to stop the impulsive words or actions that follow. She might slam her laptop shut mid-meeting, snap at a colleague, or retreat entirely and ignore messages for days. These aren't just "bad" moments, but part of a neurological loop that many people with ADHD face. It's the cycle of emotional dysregulation, impulsivity, and shame.

Anger, like all emotions, is fundamentally human. It's not "bad" or "negative" on its own. It's information that tells us when something feels unfair, our boundaries are crossed, or we're overwhelmed. But the way we *respond* to anger determines its impact. In Melissa's case, the physiological intensity of her anger, common among people with ADHD, is compounded by her brain's difficulty regulating emotional arousal and resisting impulsive urges. She often reacts before she has time to think. And once the angry behavior happens, regret and shame flood in, triggering more stress, and the cycle starts all over again.

In short, for people with ADHD, intense emotions like anger are harder to manage. Instead of processing the emotion calmly, the brain sends a fast-track message to act on it.

Positive and "Negative" Emotions: Mislabeling the Messenger

One of the greatest misconceptions in emotional health is that some feelings are inherently "bad." Emotions like anger, fear, or sadness are often labeled as negative because they're uncomfortable. In contrast, happiness, joy, or excitement are welcomed and sought after. But this binary view of emotions is misleading and unhelpful, especially for people with ADHD.

All emotions serve a function. Fear, for instance, helps us survive. Sadness can signal the need for support or reflection. Anger, while unpleasant, is a powerful signal that something needs attention—it may be injustice, personal violation, or simply internal overload. Problems arise not from the emotion itself but from the behaviors that follow when regulation is difficult.

Melissa's fear of failure, for example, doesn't become a problem until it causes her to procrastinate on financial reports or avoid clarifying misunderstandings with her boss. Her anger isn't dangerous until it pushes her to lash out or withdraw from important relationships. In other words, emotions aren't the enemy. Our *reactions* to them, particularly when distorted or dysregulated, are what can lead to negative outcomes.

Rumination and the ADHD Mind

One of the most damaging consequences of unmanaged emotions in ADHD is rumination (Kandeğer et al., 2023). Rumination is the process of continuously thinking about the same distressing events or feelings without resolution. It often masquerades as "problem-solving," but instead of leading to action, it leads to paralysis.

For Melissa, after an outburst, the thoughts start spinning: "Why did I say that? Why can't I just be normal? I've ruined everything again." These thoughts replay endlessly, like a broken record. This type of cognitive looping drains energy, deepens emotional pain, and erodes self-esteem. Research shows that rumination is strongly associated with anxiety and depression, and it's common in ADHD due to the brain's difficulty with cognitive shifting, or the ability to move attention from one idea to another. In fact, sluggish cognitive tempo (SCT) is marked by symptoms like slow physical and mental activity, frequent daydreaming, lack of motivation, and low energy. There is ongoing debate among researchers about whether SCT is a specific subtype of ADHD or a separate clinical condition altogether (Kandeğer et al., 2023).

Like Melissa, when a person fixates on the anger and their perceived failures, they aren't preparing themselves to do better next time—they're sinking deeper into hopelessness. Rumination does not teach; it punishes one's mental energy.

The Role of Cognitive Distortions in Anger

Cognitive distortions are patterns of thinking that warp our perception of reality. Everyone experiences them occasionally, but in people with ADHD, especially those struggling with emotional dysregulation, they can be constant and deeply ingrained. Some types of cognitive distortions with examples include the following (Rostain, 2025 & *Unmasking cognitive distortions*, 2025):

- **All-or-nothing thinking:** "If I'm not perfectly calm, I'm a complete failure."

- **Overgeneralization:** "I lost my temper today. I always screw up."

- **Catastrophizing:** "This one mistake will cost me my job."

- **Mind reading:** "My coworkers must think I'm unstable."

- **Emotional reasoning:** "I feel hopeless, so things must actually be hopeless."

- **Mental filtering:** Ignoring positive feedback and focusing only on the criticism.

- **Labeling:** "I'm just a terrible person."

- **Fortune telling:** "There's no way I'll ever get better."

These distortions aren't just unpleasant; they could be disabling for many. They turn temporary emotional states into fixed self-identities. They make every setback feel permanent and every mistake feel defining.

In ADHD, these thought patterns are often intensified by a lifetime of external criticism, internalized failure, and the chronic stress of navigating a world not built for neurodivergent minds. And when emotions like anger hit, these distortions become louder, more convincing, and more destructive.

Emotional Dysregulation and Impulsivity: A Neurological Double Bin d

Emotional dysregulation in ADHD isn't just having "big feelings." It's about how those feelings flood the nervous system and overwhelm executive functioning. The brain's ability to pause, reflect, and choose a helpful response is often short-circuited. Anger feels so urgent that waiting even ten seconds before reacting seems impossible.

Impulse control is already a core challenge in ADHD, but when paired with intense emotion, it becomes a combustible mix. That's why anger often leads to impulsive actions like yelling, quitting, breaking things, or saying things that can't be taken back. These impulsive behaviors often have lasting consequences, which then feed shame—and that shame becomes the emotional trigger for the next blowup.

For instance, after an angry episode at work, a person might avoid checking their email for days out of dread. This only increases stress, and when they finally open it and see a client complaint or missed deadline, their shame morphs back into anger—at herself, or at the world, and the cycle resumes.

Self-Sabotage: The Invisible Undercurrent

One of the more subtle and insidious effects of anger in the ADHD brain is self-sabotage (Rosier, 2024; Brown, 2024). This isn't always conscious. It can show up as procrastination, avoidance, disorganization, or even perfectionism. These behaviors often stem from a deep sense of inadequacy and the fear of being exposed as incapable.

After an angry episode, you might tell yourself, "There's no point in trying anymore—I always screw it up." Thus, you may avoid preparing for the next meeting. Or one might try to overcompensate by staying up late, perfecting a report, and burning themselves out in the process. These aren't isolated behaviors, but protective mechanisms, maladaptively trying to manage distress.

But the more a person self-sabotages, the more evidence they will believe they have that they're doomed to fail. The

Impulse and Fire

reality is that emotional dysregulation, and not laziness or irresponsibility, is at the root of it. Until that's addressed with compassion and understanding, the pattern will continue.

Breaking the Pattern: Challenging the Anger-Impulsivity Loop

Emotions, including anger, are a natural part of the human experience. They're not the enemy. What often leads to distress and dysfunction is not the presence of emotion itself but how we react to it, especially in individuals with ADHD, where emotional dysregulation and impulsivity often go hand-in-hand.

The good news is that the brain is capable of change. Emotional regulation is not something a person either has or doesn't have; it's a skill that can be learned and strengthened over time. Even when emotional responses feel overwhelming or out of control, it's possible to intervene, pause, and make a more intentional choice. The goal is not to stop feeling anger or sadness, but to reduce the emotional intensity and take back control over behavior.

Dealing With Emotional Dysregulation

One way to deal with emotional dysregulation could be to follow the five steps outlined below (Richard, 2022).

Step 1: Recognize the Emotion

The first step toward breaking the cycle is recognizing the early signs of emotional escalation. These signs include bodily cues like a tight chest, clenched fists, or shallow breathing; mental signals like racing thoughts, or black-and-white thinking; and behavioral urges such as snapping at others, storming off, or shutting down.

Developing this awareness takes practice. Tools like emotional tracking journals, body scans, or daily reflection can help. By identifying patterns like what emotions show up, when, and in response to what triggers, it becomes easier to anticipate and prepare for them.

Step 2: Downregulate Rather Than Escalate

Once an emotion like anger is recognized, the next step is to downregulate it—to calm the nervous system before it drives impulsive behavior. This means choosing thoughts and actions that soothe rather than inflame.

Examples of downregulating strategies include the following:

- **Reframing the situation:** Remind yourself that people make mistakes and that not everything is personal.

- **Focusing on compassionate thoughts:** Think about a time the other person was kind or helpful.

- **Grounding techniques:** Use deep breathing, progressive muscle relaxation, or five-senses grounding to return to the present.

- **Labeling the emotion:** Simply saying, "I'm feeling angry right now," can reduce emotional intensity and provide space for reflection.

The key is to minimize the narrative that fuels the anger, like interpreting someone's behavior as intentional harm, and replacing it with a more balanced perspective.

Step 3: Recognize the Impact of Emotions on Behavior

Unchecked anger often influences behavior in ways that harm relationships, self-esteem, and long-term goals. It may lead to impulsive decisions, harsh words, or withdrawal. Emotional awareness allows us to observe these patterns and realize that behavior influenced by dysregulated emotion does not define character and that it reflects a moment of overwhelm.

Tracking how emotions affect decisions and actions can help in choosing different behaviors next time. Emotional intelligence is the skill of noticing the emotion and deciding, "This doesn't have to dictate how I act."

Step 4: Accept the Emotion Without Suppressing It

Emotional acceptance is allowing feelings to exist without trying to fight, fix, or deny them. Suppressing emotions tends to intensify them over time. Acceptance reduces their power.

Acknowledging anger, without acting on it, can be as simple as pausing to say, "This is a tough moment. I'm feeling frustrated and overwhelmed." This validation creates a small but powerful shift in experiencing emotions without acting impulsively.

Step 5: Choose Where to Focus and How to Respond

Once emotions are acknowledged, it's possible to redirect attention and energy to something constructive. Don't confuse this with ignoring the emotion. You are, instead, choosing not to feed the feeling.

Redirecting could include engaging in a productive task, exercising, listening to music, or reaching out to a supportive friend. These intentional actions lessen the hold the emotion has on the mind and body.

In relationships, it may mean saying, "I need some space to calm down before we talk," instead of reacting in the heat of the moment. Over time, this practice rewires the brain to create a pause between emotion and response.

Using the Situation → Attention → Appraisal → Response Framework

This evidence-based emotional regulation strategy (Richard, 2022) helps disrupt impulsive reactions:

1. **Situation:** What triggered the emotion? Can you modify the environment to avoid or reduce exposure to the trigger? (e.g., turning off notifications, stepping away from an argument, or avoiding emotionally loaded content when stressed.)

2. **Attention:** Where is your focus? Are you mentally replaying a perceived insult or failure? Shifting attention away from the trigger can reduce its impact.

3. **Appraisal:** How are you interpreting the situation? Are you making assumptions or catastrophizing? Reassess whether your conclusion is based on facts or feelings.

4. **Response:** What response will serve your values and goals? Choose to wait, breathe, reflect, or seek support before reacting.

Breaking Self-Sabotaging Patterns

Self-sabotage often stems from the same emotional loops—anger at oneself, perfectionism, fear of failure, or internalized criticism. These responses can lead to avoidance, procrastination, and impulsive choices that undercut long-term progress.

To break this cycle (Saline, 2022), do the following:

- **Identify self-sabotaging thoughts:** "I can't do anything right," or "Why bother trying?"

Impulse and Fire

- **Challenge them with compassionate and factual rebuttals:** "I've made progress in the past," or "One mistake doesn't define my ability."

- **Set small, low-risk behavioral goals:** These "experiments" help build self-efficacy and reduce pressure.

- **Adjust expectations:** Understand that setbacks are part of learning, not proof of failure.

- **Separate identity from symptoms:** ADHD or emotional dysregulation may explain behaviors, but they are not a reflection of personal worth.

Using a growth mindset, focus on learning and progress rather than perfection. Self-compassion is essential in rewiring these patterns.

Meeting the Five Basic Needs to Support Emotional Regulation

Emotion regulation is also influenced by whether basic psychological and physiological needs are being met. These include (Rosier, 2024) the following:

1. **Survival:** Ensure you get adequate sleep, nutrition, hydration, and movement. A dysregulated body is more prone to dysregulated emotions.

2. **Power:** Seek ways to build autonomy and control over your environment or schedule, even in small ways.

3. **Love:** Cultivate connection and self-acceptance. Practice affirmations and reach out for support when needed.

4. **Fun:** Schedule activities that bring enjoyment and laughter. Play reduces stress and restores emotional balance.

5. **Freedom:** Give yourself choices where possible. Feeling trapped fuels emotional reactivity; autonomy supports regulation.

Even when emotional dysregulation feels automatic, it's possible to create a gap between stimulus and response. Within that gap lies one's choice and the opportunity to build new patterns that support healthier and more empowered emotional lives.

Key Takeaways

While looking at ADHD rage patterns in this chapter, we have also explored some preliminary ways of breaking those patterns. One of the primary ways of beginning this journey is through combating negative thought patterns or cognitive distortions. We must also remember that these steps can't achieve anything overnight and require consistent effort and practice.

In the next chapter, we will look at one important way to calm ourselves for the long haul—mindfulness-based intervention and strategies.

Self-Reflection

Whenever you are met with unhelpful thoughts that you recognize as cognitive distortions, ask yourself:

- What evidence do I have that supports or contradicts this thought?

- Am I assuming the worst without proof?

- Would I say this to a friend in my position?

- Is this thought based on facts or feelings?

- What's a more compassionate or realistic way to see this?

- Am I mentally stuck in the past or projecting into the future?

- What am I avoiding by staying stuck in this thought?

- Can I do one small thing right now to shift my focus or energy?

- What need is this thought trying to meet?

Chapter 8

The Power of Mindfulness— Calming the ADHD Brain

What Is Mindfulness?

Mindfulness is the practice of consciously bringing one's attention to the present moment with openness, curiosity, and nonjudgment. At its core, it involves developing an acute awareness of our internal states, such as thoughts, emotions, and bodily sensations, as well as our external environment, without immediately judging or reacting to them (*Mindfulness*, 2022). While the concept has deep roots in Eastern philosophy, particularly within traditions such as ancient Chinese and Buddhist medicine, mindfulness has been widely adapted into modern Western psychology over the past few decades (Sutton, 2019). Its therapeutic value has been recognized and incorporated into clinical programs such as mindfulness-based stress reduction (MBSR), mindfulness-based cognitive therapy (MBCT), and dialectical behavior therapy (DBT).

The purpose of mindfulness is not to empty the mind or suppress thoughts and emotions, but rather to create a space between stimulus and response. In that space lies the power to choose how we react, what we say, and how we act. For individuals with attention-deficit/hyperactivity disorder (ADHD), particularly those prone to emotional dysregulation and rage, this practice offers an evidence-based route to greater self-control, improved attention, and emotional resilience.

Psychologist and mindfulness researcher, Dr. Shauna Shapiro, identifies three core components essential to effective mindfulness practice, which are intention, attention, and attitude (Sutton, 2019). Intention refers to our personal purpose for being mindful, often guided by deeper values such as healing, compassion, or self-awareness. Attention is the act of focusing deliberately on present-moment experience. Furthermore, attitude reflects how we pay attention, ideally with kindness, patience, and curiosity rather than self-judgment or criticism.

The Neuroscience of Mindfulness

Mindfulness is not just a philosophical concept; it is a neurological practice that can lead to measurable changes in neural structure and function. For individuals with ADHD and difficulties managing intense anger, understanding the underlying neuroscience can be both validating and motivating. Brain imaging studies using fMRI and EEG have provided growing evidence that mindfulness significantly affects regions of the brain responsible for attention, self-regulation, and emotional processing, all areas commonly impaired in ADHD.

One of the key findings in neuroscience is that mindfulness activates the prefrontal cortex, a brain region essential for executive functioning, including decision-making, impulse control, and metacognition—the ability to think about one's own thinking. Research also suggests that mindfulness meditation may positively benefit other regions of the brain including the somatomotor cortex, insula, hippocampus, anterior cingulate cortex (ACC), and orbitofrontal cortex (OFC) (Wang, n.d.). Both cross-sectional and longitudinal studies have found that experienced meditators exhibit increased brain activation and structural changes in various parts of the brain (Tang, 2017), suggesting that mindfulness can help train the brain for better focus and self-monitoring. When individuals practice mindfulness, particularly through focused attention meditations, they engage these higher-order brain functions. Over time, this activation may lead to structural and functional improvements in this region, supporting greater self-awareness and behavioral control.

Emotion regulation is another area where mindfulness exerts powerful effects. Long-term mindfulness practitioners have shown enhanced connectivity in brain regions responsible for regulating negative emotions (Kral et al., 2018), including the amygdala, which governs the body's fear and stress responses. Regular mindfulness practice has been associated with a decrease in amygdala reactivity, leading to lower levels of stress, anxiety, and emotional volatility—benefits that are particularly relevant for managing ADHD rage.

Mindfulness can impact another important area, the default mode network (DMN). The DMN is active when the brain is at rest and not focused on the outside world, essentially when we're daydreaming, ruminating, or caught in self-referential thoughts. In individuals with ADHD, the DMN can become hyperactive, contributing to distractibility and a sense of mental chaos. Mindfulness helps quiet the DMN, reducing rumination and allowing for a clearer, more present-centered awareness. This can help individuals break free from "autopilot" behavior and increase intentionality in their daily actions.

Interestingly, long-term mindfulness practitioners exhibit higher pain tolerance, which speaks to the broader capacity for mind-body regulation that mindfulness cultivates. By enhancing interoceptive awareness, or being more attuned to the body's internal cues, individuals can respond to discomfort, stress, or emotional triggers more skillfully, rather than reacting impulsively.

How Awareness and Focus Can Help Control Anger

As we have seen in the previous chapters, anger, particularly in individuals with ADHD, is often the product of overwhelming stimuli, impulsive reactions, and difficulty regulating emotional arousal. This anger can manifest quickly and intensely, often disproportionate to the trigger. Mindfulness helps to create a buffer zone, or a moment of conscious awareness, between the trigger and the emotional response.

Practicing mindfulness over long periods of time can strengthen two critical cognitive skills impaired in ADHD—attention regulation and emotional self-awareness. By training the mind to notice distractions without becoming entangled in them, individuals can become more aware of the initial signs of rising anger, such as muscle tension, rapid heartbeat, or intrusive thoughts, and intervene before the emotional storm escalates.

In neuroscientific terms, mindfulness practice appears to impact the DMN of the brain, which is responsible for automatic thoughts. Mindfulness seems to target the recognition of automatic thoughts in particular. While mindfulness helps increase attention, it may also help alleviate symptoms of depression, anxiety, and stress (Marchand, 2014). This recalibration of neural circuitry supports a more balanced emotional state and a reduced tendency to react impulsively. There is also compelling evidence to suggest that certain meditative practices help improve attention, especially in people with ADHD (Modesto-Lowe et al., 2015). Mindfulness has also been shown to be effective in changing negative habits or patterns of behavior like smoking or drinking (Sutton, 2019).

While mindfulness as a psychological construct is still being explored in scientific research, there is a growing body of evidence supporting its efficacy in managing ADHD symptoms. Some researchers go as far as to claim that mindfulness can bring about trait and state changes in people (Sutton, 2019). In one notable study, participants engaged in a mindfulness training program that included progressive meditation practice, starting with five-minute sessions and eventually extending to 20 minutes. Each weekly session lasted approximately 2.5 hours and included guided meditations, group discussions, and at-home assignments supported by audio recordings. The results were promising, with 78% of participants completing the study, and approximately 30% reporting a greater than 30% reduction in core ADHD symptoms such as difficulties with set shifting (switching between tasks) and conflict attention (managing competing demands) (Modesto-Lowe et al., 2015). Importantly, these improvements were not just subjective; they correlated with behavioral and neurocognitive changes linked to better self-regulation.

In addition to improving attention, mindfulness has also been shown to reduce rumination, stress, and emotional reactivity—all of which are commonly associated with ADHD rage. When individuals learn to anchor themselves in the present, they are less likely to be swept away by past frustrations or future anxieties. This groundedness can profoundly impact their ability to respond to life's challenges with calm and intention.

In learning to observe rather than suppress or act on anger, individuals can develop greater control over their behavioral responses. Instead of yelling or acting out, they can pause, acknowledge the emotion, and choose a more constructive response, such as walking away, naming the feeling, or engaging in a calming activity.

Mindfulness Beyond Meditation

It's important to note that mindfulness is often mistakenly equated solely with meditation. While meditation is one powerful form of cultivating mindfulness, it is far from the only one. In fact, mindfulness can be integrated into nearly any aspect of daily life. Whether eating a meal, taking a walk, or brushing your teeth, the key is to bring full awareness to the activity at hand, engaging the senses and observing the experience without judgment or distraction.

For people with ADHD, this approach can be especially effective. The constant internal chatter, restlessness, and impulsivity that often characterize ADHD can make formal seated meditation difficult at first. However, practicing mindfulness in movement or during routine activities offers a more accessible entry point. Over time, this kind of daily attentiveness can build the mental muscles needed to reduce reactivity and increase clarity during emotionally charged moments.

Is Mindfulness Mandatory?

While mindfulness offers a compelling array of benefits supported by neuroscience, it's important to emphasize that it is not a solution that may work for everyone. Mindfulness is certainly just one path among many, but for some, it can be a transformative tool for calming the storm of ADHD rage. Some individuals, however, find it challenging to practice consistently, while others might feel it doesn't yield immediate or sufficient benefits for the effort it requires.

There are many other effective interventions for managing ADHD and anger, including cognitive behavioral therapy (CBT), dialectical behavior therapy (DBT), medication, physical exercise, and creative therapeutic outlets such as art, music, or writing. Each of these methods offers unique pathways toward self-regulation and emotional resilience.

Ultimately, the key is to find approaches that align with your personal temperament, lifestyle, and goals. The aim isn't to force yourself into a practice that feels burdensome or unnatural. Rather, you should be working *with* yourself, gently and consistently, to create the change you want to see.

Mindfulness Practices for ADHD Rage

Mindfulness is most effective when it becomes part of a consistent, daily routine, especially for individuals with ADHD who struggle with emotional impulsivity and racing thoughts. While the idea of "sitting still and being quiet" may initially seem counterintuitive to someone with a hyperactive mind, the reality is that mindfulness isn't about emptying the brain. It's about *training your attention* and *building self-awareness*, even when your mind is noisy. With practice, this awareness becomes your superpower, or the pause between trigger and reaction that will allow you to choose how to respond, instead of being hijacked by anger.

Below are some practical, easy-to-follow mindfulness exercises designed to help calm the overactive ADHD brain and manage intense emotions like rage. Before beginning any mindfulness practice, remove any distractions, especially your phone, unless you're using it to play some guided audio. Creating a distraction-free zone helps the brain understand that this is an intentional time for self-regulation and calm.

Body Awareness /Body Scan Exercise

This exercise grounds you in your physical self, making it ideal for moments when you feel disconnected or emotionally overwhelmed. A body scan trains your mind to shift attention gently from one part of the body to another, noticing sensations without reacting or judging them.

How to practice:

- Find a quiet space to sit or lie down comfortably.

- Close your eyes and take a few deep breaths.

- Start at the top of your head and mentally "scan" down through each part of your body—forehead, eyes, jaw, neck, shoulders, arms, chest, stomach, legs, and feet.

- At each point, pause and simply notice how that area feels—tense, relaxed, numb, itchy, warm, or cool.

- Don't try to change anything. Just observe.

- If your mind drifts (which it will), gently bring it back to the body part you were scanning.

This exercise, when practiced regularly, can help you reconnect to your body's signals and intervene before emotions like anger become explosive.

Guided Breathing

Breath is one of the most powerful anchors to the present moment. It's always with you, always available, and deeply linked to your nervous system. Intentional breathing slows down your heart rate and activates the parasympathetic nervous system, calming your fight-or-flight response.

How to practice:

- Sit upright in a chair or lie down on your back.

- Inhale deeply through your nose for a count of four.

- Hold the breath for a count of two.

- Exhale slowly through your mouth for a count of six.

- Repeat for 3–5 minutes.

You can also follow a guided breathing video for structure. Just remember that the goal isn't to "do it perfectly" but to notice your breath and to gently bring back your attention when it wanders.

Mindful Minute

This is a short but powerful reset tool for ADHD minds in moments of frustration or irritation. Even one minute of focused awareness can interrupt a rising wave of anger and help you make a conscious choice instead of reacting impulsively.

How to practice:

- Set a timer for 60 seconds.

- Sit or stand still and choose one point of focus—your breath, the feeling of your feet on the floor, or a sound in the room.

- Keep your attention there. When thoughts pull you away, acknowledge them without judgment and return to your chosen focus.

- After the minute ends, take a deep breath and return to your task with greater clarity.

Use this technique as an "emotional reset button" during your day, especially before responding to an upsetting situation.

Listening to Nature Sounds

Natural sounds like birdsong, rainfall, or ocean waves are inherently soothing to the nervous system. They encourage relaxation and presence without requiring you to "do" anything. For ADHD individuals who struggle to sit still or focus during formal meditation, this passive form of mindfulness can be very effective.

How to practice:

- Find a quiet place where you can sit undisturbed.

- Play nature sounds through headphones or a speaker, preferably something rhythmic like rain, waves, or wind.

- Close your eyes and listen with full attention. Notice how the sound moves, rises, and falls.

- If your mind starts to wander or you begin thinking about tasks, just acknowledge the thought and come back to the sound.

This exercise is especially helpful before bed or after a stressful day to ease the mind into a calmer state.

Mountain Meditation

The mountain meditation is a guided visualization that cultivates emotional stability and inner strength. By imagining yourself as a grounded, unmoving mountain, you can create an internal sense of resilience, perfect for moments when you feel like you're about to erupt with rage.

How to practice:

- Sit in a comfortable position with your back straight.

- Close your eyes and imagine a mountain—tall, unmoving, enduring all seasons.

- Now imagine you are that mountain, your body still and grounded, and your mind observing clouds (thoughts and emotions) passing overhead.

- The weather changes with storms (anger), sun (joy), or wind (anxiety) passing by, but the mountain remains.

This metaphor can help reframe how you relate to your emotions. You're not the storm—you're the mountain beneath it.

Urge Surfing

Urge surfing is a mindfulness technique that helps you ride out intense emotional or behavioral impulses without acting on them. Think of the urge to explode in anger like a wave; it rises, peaks, and eventually passes. You can't stop the wave, but you can choose not to get wiped out by it.

How to practice:

- The next time you feel a powerful emotion rising (rage, frustration), pause and name the urge silently: *"I feel the urge to yell."*

- Notice where you feel it in your body—tight chest, clenched fists, racing thoughts, etc.

- Imagine the urge to be a wave. Watch it rise, peak, and slowly fall.

- Focus on your breath as the anchor. Breathe through the discomfort.

- Remind yourself: *"This is temporary. I don't have to act on it."*

Practicing urge surfing regularly builds emotional tolerance and rewires impulsive patterns.

Key Takeaways

If you are looking for nonmedical ways to manage emotions and feel emotionally resilient, mindfulness could be an extremely powerful tool. However, not everything works for everyone. There are as many people who swear by mindfulness as there are who can't seem to benefit from it.

In the next chapter, we will look at the psychological tools that are most often recommended for ADHD and emotional dysregulation.

Self-Reflection

Try each of the exercises above over the coming weeks. Notice which ones resonate with you and which ones feel challenging. Adapt them as needed. The goal is not to suppress your ADHD brain, but to work with it, teaching it to slow down just enough so you can steer, rather than spin out of control.

Chapter 9

Cognitive Behavioral Tools for Managing Anger

Leticia was a 44-year-old senior midwife working in one of the busiest maternity wards in the city. She was known for her precision, efficiency, and unflinching attitude in high-pressure situations. However, she was also known for her temper. Her colleagues walked on eggshells around her. First-time mothers sometimes left her care in tears, describing her as cold or even cruel. One patient, terrified by Leticia's raised voice during labor, filed a formal complaint. It wasn't the first.

When the hospital administration gave her an ultimatum—mandatory therapy or permanent suspension, Leticia agreed reluctantly. "Therapy's just emotional indulgence for people who can afford to fall apart," she told her assigned therapist during their first session. Her arms were crossed tightly, and her eyes unblinking.

It took weeks for Leticia to admit vulnerability. Raised in a home where emotions were a luxury she couldn't afford, she had learned to bury her own feelings under duty and survival. Her mother died of cancer when Leticia was 16. Her father,

Impulse and Fire

an angry alcoholic, disappeared into barrooms and left her to raise her three younger siblings. She became "the little general," holding everything together in the house. Crying wasn't allowed, and she internalized that weakness got people hurt. She learned to be tough and emotionally untouchable. That armor had gotten her through medical training, her divorce, and single parenthood.

Her therapist, sensing that traditional cognitive therapy might not reach her hardened defenses, took an unconventional route—compassion-focused therapy. He gently introduced the idea that her anger was a survival strategy and not a flaw. Through guided exercises, Leticia explored the idea of three emotional systems—threat, drive, and soothing. Her threat alert system had been working nonstop for thirty years, always bracing for disaster, while the soothing system, meant for rest, connection, and healing, was a stranger to her.

When asked to visualize a protective figure that made her feel safe, Leticia chose a jaguar, which to her symbolized strength, silence, and lethality. That image became her grounding image during moments when rage began to rise in her like a tidal wave.

Still, Leticia's anger was both psychological and physical. It was stored in her muscles, her joints, and her jaw. During one particularly tense session, she described how her hands felt electrified before she exploded. The therapist referred her to trauma-sensitive yoga and somatic therapy, which she approached with skepticism. However, as she began to move and breathe differently, she noticed memories surfacing—of nights sleeping by the door to guard her siblings, and suppressing screams when her father slammed kitchen drawers at 2 a.m. Her body, it seemed, remembered everything her mind had silenced.

In a session halfway through the year, Leticia mentioned that she used to love photography. She'd dreamed of capturing birth, not just the act of it, but the raw, quiet moments that followed. Her therapist encouraged her to reclaim that part of herself. Tentatively at first, Leticia began taking photos again. She snapped shots of sterile delivery rooms between shifts, empty bassinets, and sunlight spilling over hospital floors. Eventually, she asked the hospital for permission to photograph staff and patients, anonymously, as part of a project she called *The Quiet Hour*. The photos captured the unspeakable moments of joy, grief, exhaustion, and intimacy. Leticia submitted a few to an internal wellness initiative, and they became part of a rotating exhibit.

Something softened in her. Her rage, once volcanic, became a simmer. She didn't fully understand her own transformation until she attended a support group for medical professionals dealing with burnout. There, surrounded by exhausted nurses and bitter surgeons, Leticia found words she hadn't known she needed: "I'm not angry at my patients," she confessed. "I'm angry that no one ever cared for *me* the way I care for them."

The silence that followed was not awkward, but reverent. For the first time, she cried in front of others, not out of shame, but out of relief.

After 10 months of therapy, Leticia was reinstated at work with no further incidents. When difficult emotions did arise, she used breathwork and visualization to ground herself. Leticia had finally made space for softness.

***

Some Conventional and Nonconventional Therapies and Treatments Prescribed for ADHD and Emotional Dysregulation

We have looked at the effects of rage in personal and professional lives several times in this book. Now, let's look at some of the most effective strategies in curbing it.

Cognitive Behavioral Therapy (CBT)

CBT (What is cognitive behavioral therapy?, 2017 & Toohey, 2021) is a structured, goal-oriented form of psychotherapy that has proven highly effective in helping individuals with ADHD manage emotional challenges (Knouse & Safren, 2010), especially anger. For those with ADHD, intense emotions often arise quickly and feel overwhelming. Anger may erupt in response to frustration, perceived rejection, or even minor setbacks. CBT provides practical tools to help individuals pause, reflect, and respond more constructively.

A core element of CBT is learning to identify cognitive distortions or automatic, often exaggerated thoughts that fuel emotional reactivity (McIntyre et al., 2019). People with ADHD may experience distorted thinking like "I always mess things up" or "No one respects me," which can escalate into frustration or rage. Through CBT, individuals are taught how to catch these thoughts, evaluate their accuracy, and replace them with more balanced alternatives, such as "This was a mistake, not a failure," or "I can handle this situation calmly."

CBT also emphasizes reframing anger. Instead of reacting impulsively to perceived threats or disappointments, individuals learn to reframe their internal dialogue using calming and supportive self-talk. Techniques such as breathing exercises, mindfulness, and visualization are often integrated into sessions, helping the individual build emotional regulation skills that can be used in daily life.

Beyond emotional control, CBT supports practical skills that can reduce the stressors that often lead to anger. Time management, organizational strategies, and social communication skills are woven into the treatment, helping the individual manage ADHD-related chaos that might otherwise spark irritability. As daily frustrations decrease and coping skills improve, a person will be able to gain self-esteem, making angry outbursts less frequent and less intense.

CBT is not intended to suppress emotion but rather to understand its roots and respond with intention rather than impulse. For individuals with ADHD, this approach creates a clear path toward calmer reactions, healthier relationships, and a more balanced emotional life.

Dialectical Behavior Therapy (DBT)

While DBT was originally developed to treat borderline personality disorder (Ramsay, 2018), it has increasingly shown value in helping individuals with ADHD, especially those who struggle with intense emotions and impulsive reactions, such as frequent bouts of anger. DBT combines traditional behavioral techniques with mindfulness and acceptance strategies, making it particularly effective in teaching people how to manage emotional intensity and improve their relationships.

One of DBT's key strengths is its structured approach to developing emotion regulation skills. Individuals with ADHD often experience emotional dysregulation, where feelings such as anger, shame, or frustration flare up rapidly and intensely. DBT helps individuals recognize their emotional triggers, understand the buildup of emotional responses, and apply calming strategies before reaching a breaking point. This shift from reactive to responsive behavior can significantly reduce rage episodes and improve daily functioning.

Mindfulness, a core component of DBT, teaches individuals to be present in the moment and observe their emotions without judgment. This skill allows someone with ADHD to pause, acknowledge what they're feeling, and create space between the emotion and the reaction. For example, rather than lashing out in anger, the person can recognize the emotion, take a breath, and choose a calmer response.

Another essential area of DBT is distress tolerance, which includes impulsivity management. Individuals learn to "check the facts" before reacting, apply techniques like deep breathing or grounding exercises, and use skills like Stop, Take a step back, Observe, and Proceed mindfully (STOP) to slow down impulsive responses. These strategies empower individuals to regain control during emotionally charged moments.

DBT also focuses on interpersonal effectiveness, helping individuals with ADHD navigate social situations more smoothly. Skills such as assertive communication, conflict resolution, and boundary-setting help improve relationships and reduce frustration in personal and professional interactions.

In individual therapy, clients work one-on-one with a therapist to process their experiences, apply DBT skills to real-life challenges, and develop greater self-awareness. In some settings, case management is also incorporated, helping clients build executive functioning and learn how to manage their lives more independently, which is critical for people with ADHD who may struggle with organization and follow-through.

Ultimately, while CBT aims to shift negative thought patterns, DBT places emphasis on managing emotions and accepting feelings while still promoting change. For individuals with ADHD, DBT offers a compassionate, skills-based approach to taming anger, reducing stress, and building a more stable and fulfilling emotional life.

Research has established that a structured CBT/DBT approach can improve symptoms associated with ADHD, such as depression, interpersonal difficulties, low self-esteem, and low quality of life, especially among those who show little to no response to medication for the same (Cole et al., 2016). Another study found that patients who engaged in weekly DBT-group treatment for ADHD found improvement in their executive functioning and other symptoms as compared to those who adopted treatment as usual. These results also sustained for six months after the treatment ended (Halmøy et al., 2022). A third study also established DBT's positive influence in assuaging the emotional difficulties associated with ADHD (Basiri, 2025).

The Role of Medication in Managing ADHD and Anger

While therapy is essential for building long-term emotional regulation skills, medication can play a key supportive role in managing ADHD-related anger and impulsivity (*ADHD Medications*, 2022; McMillen et al., 2024). For many, medication helps create a more stable internal environment, making it easier to apply the strategies learned through CBT or DBT.

Stimulant medications are the most commonly prescribed treatment for ADHD. They work by increasing the levels of dopamine and norepinephrine, two neurotransmitters that are often imbalanced in populations with ADHD. These chemicals help improve attention, focus, and impulse control, which in turn can reduce the intensity and frequency of emotional outbursts. For someone who struggles with quick-trigger anger, stimulants can provide the mental "brakes" needed to pause before reacting.

Non-stimulant medications offer an alternative for individuals who don't respond well to stimulants or are at risk for misuse.

These medications, which also target norepinephrine levels, may take longer to show effects but can be equally effective in improving attention and reducing emotional volatility. Importantly, because they are not classified as controlled substances, they carry a lower risk of dependence.

Antidepressants are sometimes used "off-label" to treat ADHD, particularly in individuals who also struggle with mood disorders or anxiety. These medications can help stabilize mood and reduce irritability by acting on both dopamine and norepinephrine levels. While not FDA-approved specifically for ADHD, they can be part of a well-rounded treatment plan under a provider's supervision.

Since medication can come with its own share of side effects in some patients, it is important to note that any drug discussed above should be taken only under the prescription of a qualified healthcare professional.

Some Alternative ADHD Therapies

While traditional therapies and medication form the foundation of ADHD treatment, nontraditional approaches (*ADHD Alternative Treatments*, 2025; *ADHD and Complementary Health Approaches*, 2023; *Alternative Treatments for Attention Deficit Hyperactivity Disorder*, 2003; White, n.d.) can offer additional support, especially in managing anger and improving emotional balance. These complementary therapies address physical, mental, and creative dimensions of health, contributing to a more holistic management strategy.

- **Exercise** is one of the most accessible and effective tools for individuals with ADHD. Physical activity boosts dopamine, norepinephrine, and serotonin levels, many of the same neurotransmitters targeted by ADHD medications. Regular movement, whether running, swimming, dancing, or even brisk walking, can improve mood, reduce impulsivity, and help regulate frustration and anger. Many people with ADHD report feeling calmer and more focused after exercising.

- **Diet** is a more debated area, but a generally healthy, balanced diet supports overall well-being and energy regulation. Some studies suggest that polyunsaturated fatty acids, like omega-3s found in fish oil, may provide mild benefits for ADHD symptoms, particularly attention and mood regulation. Melatonin supplements have shown some success in improving the quality and duration of sleep. Removing specific food groups from the diet, such as gluten or sugars, should be approached with caution, as they may also lead to a lack of proper nutrient intake as well. While diet alone is not a cure, proper nutrition can prevent blood sugar crashes and nutritional deficiencies that might worsen symptoms like irritability.

- **Creative therapies** like art, music, dance, and writing offer powerful outlets for emotional expression (Kariž, 2003; *Art Therapy in the Treatment of Attention Deficit Hyperactivity Disorder*, 2021). These are especially helpful for children with ADHD, who may struggle to articulate feelings verbally. In group settings, these therapies also promote social connection, emotional safety, and self-awareness, which are key components in managing anger.

- **Sleep** is critically important. ADHD is strongly linked to poor sleep patterns, though it's not clear whether ADHD causes sleep issues or vice versa. Improving sleep, through consistent routines, reduced screen time, and healthy sleep hygiene, could significantly reduce emotional volatility and impulsivity.

- **Biofeedback,** and more specifically **neurofeedback,** uses real-time feedback on physiological functions like brainwaves to help individuals gain control over stress responses and improve focus by training their minds. Early research suggests it may help with attention, emotional regulation, and executive functioning.

- Finally, **working memory training**, often delivered through computer-based programs, can help strengthen short-term memory and cognitive flexibility. While not a standalone solution, it can support better focus and frustration tolerance.

Integrating these nontraditional approaches with structured therapy and professional guidance creates a richer, more personalized path toward emotional stability and anger management for individuals with ADHD.

Everyday Strategies for Anger Management in ADHD

Managing anger in ADHD requires a blend of awareness, preparation, and consistent behavioral strategies. One of the most effective techniques is to break anger management into step-by-step actions that reduce reactivity. For instance, you can begin by identifying your common triggers or situations, environments, or people that tend to ignite your anger. Once recognized, you can plan constructive responses, like stepping away, using deep breathing, or journaling your thoughts before reacting.

Minimizing distractions and temptations also plays a key role. For example, if impulsive spending triggers frustration, limit access to credit cards and carry only a certain amount of necessary cash. If social settings lead to poor decisions, like drinking or arguing, choose alternate environments that support calm behavior.

Shift your internal dialogue by replacing negative self-talk with neutral or encouraging alternatives. Statements like "I'm failing again" can be reframed as "I'm having a tough moment, and I can handle it." Over time, this reduces emotional escalation.

Consider maintaining healthy habits like regular sleep, nutritious meals, daily movement, and engaging hobbies, all of which support emotional resilience.

Most importantly, don't hesitate to seek professional help. Combining CBT or DBT with appropriate medication can reduce ADHD symptoms, including anger, and build long-term emotional regulation. With time and effort, real and long-term change is possible. You can also check out the course on anger management on Impulsivity.com for more daily tips to keep your rage in check.

Key Takeaways

In this chapter, we looked at some of the conventional and established therapeutic strategies that are used to manage ADHD and its related symptoms. We also looked over an arsenal of tools that are available at one's disposal. However, ultimately, each person's experiences are unique, and what they choose should be a method or combination of methods that will yield results for them specifically.

In the next chapter, we will explore some practical daily steps to build impulse control in our lives.

Self-Reflection

- **understanding my anger**

    - What are the most common triggers leading to my anger or emotional outbursts?

    - How does my anger typically show up—physically, emotionally, or behaviorally?

   Impulse and Fire

- **cognitive patterns**

  - What negative or distorted thoughts do I often have before I get angry?

  - Can I identify times when changing my thoughts helped de-escalate a situation?

- **therapeutic tools**

  - What CBT or DBT strategies have I found helpful, or would I be willing to try?

  - How has mindfulness, breathing, or reframing thoughts helped me in moments of stress?

- **habits and lifestyle**

  - Am I consistently sleeping, eating, and exercising in ways that support my emotional regulation?

  - Which lifestyle habits tend to make my anger worse? Which ones help reduce it?

- **creative and alternative outlets**

  - Do I have creative or physical outlets (like art, writing, dance, or exercise) that help me express and manage my emotions?

  - How often do I make time for hobbies or activities that bring me joy?

- **support system and accountability**

  - Do I have a therapist, coach, or support group I can turn to when I'm struggling?

  - How comfortable am I with asking for help when I feel overwhelmed?

- **medication and professional care**

  - Have I spoken to a qualified professional about whether medication might help me manage my ADHD and related anger?

  - If I'm on medication, am I tracking its effects and communicating openly with my provider?

- **behavioral awareness**

  - What steps can I take to reduce exposure to temptations or triggers in my environment?

  - When I reflect on recent episodes of anger, what would I do differently now?

Chapter 10

Strategies for Impulse Control—Building Emotional Resilience

Anger in individuals with ADHD often explodes without warning, not necessarily because they want to react that way, but because their brains are wired for immediacy. To understand and manage ADHD rage, the first crucial step is understanding impulse control, the neurological mechanism that allows us to pause before reacting.

Understanding Impulse Control

What Is Impulse Control?

Impulse control is a function of the brain's executive system, particularly involving the prefrontal cortex, which governs decision-making, judgment, and emotional regulation. In ADHD, this system is often underactive or delayed in its activation. As a result, the "fight-or-flight" centers in the brain, like the amygdala, can overpower rational thought before self-restraint kicks in. This leads to immediate, often disproportionate, emotional responses, which we might recognize as ADHD rage.

How to Delay Immediate Reactions

While it may feel like emotions hijack the brain in milliseconds, developing techniques to insert a brief delay between feeling and reacting can be life-changing. This delay allows us to think before we leap into action.

One of the most effective tools for this is building a "cooling off" routine, which can include the following:

- **Deep breathing:** This step activates the parasympathetic nervous system and calms the body by combating the stress hormones being released. This will also help your heart rate return to normal.

- **Slowing down:** Reminding yourself to take a break, or revisit a problem after you've had the time to cool down, will help you pause the act button. Identifying what you're feeling (e.g., "I feel frustrated") will help reduce the intensity of feelings and create distance, fostering emotional regulation and well-being.

- **Thinking outside the box:** This is vital to ensure we don't get stuck in our own perspective at the exclusion of other people's feelings, points of view, and emotions.

- **Pause-stop-rewind-fast forward-play:** Pause to consider all the options available in the situation. Stop an action that you know will create trouble. Rewind to think of times you have already made this or a similar decision before. Fast forward to consider the consequences of your actions. Finally, play only when you are really ready to act.

Impulse and Fire

The Marshmallow Test and the Science of Delayed Gratification

The famous Stanford marshmallow test (Navidad, 2023), in which children were offered one marshmallow right away or two if they waited, has become a symbol of self-regulation and delayed gratification. Though the results are debatable, it has generally been understood that children who could wait for two marshmallows later instead of eating the one before them had better outcomes in emotional regulation, academic achievement, and stress management later in life.

However, this doesn't mean impulse control is a trait you are either born with or not. It can be trained. In ADHD, delaying gratification helps weaken the intensity of the original impulse. If you can learn to wait, even just five seconds, the emotional heat begins to dissipate. You can think of it like pulling a pot off a burner. The longer it sits away from the stove, the cooler it becomes. The more times you learn to wait before reacting to triggers, the more "cooling off" will become a habitual trait.

Mindfulness as a Cooling Mechanism

As we have seen in earlier chapters, an evidence-based tool for improving impulse control is mindfulness. In people with ADHD, mindfulness can

- improve attention regulation.

- reduce emotional reactivity.

- increase the ability to pause before reacting.

We have covered quite a few mindfulness exercises in Chapter 8. Below is another technique you can practice if you feel mindfulness is your cup of tea.

Quick Mindfulness Exercise: The "RAIN" Technique

The **RAIN** technique (Brach, n.d.) is a powerful tool for managing intense emotions like rage. Developed by mindfulness teachers such as Tara Brach, it's rooted in evidence-based practices that improve emotional regulation and impulse control.

- **R–Recognize:** Identify what you are feeling in the moment. For example, "I'm feeling furious right now." This helps to downregulate emotional intensity.

- **A–Allow:** Accept that the emotion is present without trying to fight it or act on it. For instance, "This is how I feel, and that's okay. I don't need to fix it immediately." This reduces internal resistance, which can often intensify emotional reactions.

- **I–Investigate:** Bring gentle curiosity to the feeling. Where is it in your body? What triggered it? For example, "My chest is tight. My jaw is clenched. I felt disrespected." This step helps distance yourself from the emotion, turning the experience into something you're *observing*, rather than something you *are*.

- **N–Nurture:** Offer compassion to yourself. Acknowledge the difficulty of the moment and respond kindly. For example, "This is hard, and I'm doing my best. I can get through this without lashing out." Soothing the nervous system, this step helps restore emotional balance.

Related to mindfulness, we can also create our own internal pause buttons to triggers, which we shall examine below.

Creating Internal Pause Buttons

As covered earlier, tools like "slowing down," "rewinding," and "pressing pause" are crucial metaphors and mechanisms. In practice, this can look like

Impulse and Fire

- **mentally replaying a recent overreaction** and envisioning what a paused response would have looked like.

- **practicing with low-stakes situations,** like choosing to wait before responding to a mildly annoying text.

- **using visual or tactile reminders,** such as a bracelet or sticky note, to trigger a pause.

These "pause buttons" must be practiced frequently to become automatic or habitual responses to triggering situations.

Importantly, long-lasting change for the better is only possible if we are truly committed to it despite the initial setbacks and challenges. As such, we are going to look at the seven stages of behavioral change you can realistically expect when you begin your journey.

The 7 Stages of Behavioral Change: How Impulse Control Evolves Over Time

Impulse control doesn't improve overnight. Like any skill, it follows the arc of the seven stages of change (Richard, 2022), a clinically supported model used in behavioral psychology.

1. **Precontemplation:** You're not yet thinking about changing your reaction patterns. You might say, "That's just how I am."

   - **Tip:** Track your emotional outbursts without judgment. Awareness is the first seed of change.

2. **Contemplation:** You begin to see a problem. You notice your rage damages relationships or self-esteem.

   - **Tip:** Write down a list of pros and cons for working on your impulse control. This builds motivation.

3. **Planning or preparation:** You're ready to act and are gathering strategies. You might be reading this book or talking to a therapist.

   - **Tip:** Choose one tool (like the STOP technique) to try daily for a week.

4. **Implementation or action:** You're actively working on your behavior. You're pausing, breathing, and practicing mindfulness in real-time.

   - **Tip:** Keep a journal of success moments, no matter how small. These build neural reinforcement.

5. **Maintenance:** You've made progress and are sustaining it. You might still feel the impulse, but you're learning to sit with it.

   - **Tip:** Continue mindfulness practice and revisit what worked in past flare-ups.

6. **Lapse:** You have a setback. You yelled again or acted out of rage. This is normal.

   - **Tip:** Don't aim to start over. Instead, reflect, repair, and re-engage. Ask yourself, "What was different this time?"

7. **Relapse:** Old patterns might return more frequently. This may happen under stress or if supports are removed.

   - **Tip:** Return to the basics. What helped in the beginning? Reconnect with accountability structures like therapy or support groups.

Understanding and managing ADHD rage is not about stopping emotions, but learning to ride the wave without crashing. Each moment you delay, breathe, and choose differently, you build the neurological and emotional muscles needed for lasting change.

Strength From Within: Building Emotional Resilience

Rage often feels like a wave that knocks you down, but resilience can help you get back up, calmer, clearer, and more in control. In the context of ADHD and anger management, emotional resilience is not about avoiding challenges altogether, but rather enduring them better, learning from them, and growing stronger in the process.

What Is Emotional Resilience?

Emotional resilience is the capacity to bounce back from setbacks, regulate intense feelings, and adapt positively to stress or adversity. It's not something you either have or don't have, but a skillset that can be developed over time, especially with intentional practice.

Why It Matters

Research has consistently shown that resilience is associated with greater happiness, lower rates of depression and anxiety, stronger immune function, and better physical health. In one longitudinal study, children who thrived despite being exposed to significant adversity like poverty, abuse, and family dysfunction were found to have high levels of internal and external protective factors. This is the foundation of resilience.

Risk Factors and Resilience

We all carry certain risk factors that increase vulnerability to emotional distress and rage outbursts:

- Some risk factors are within our control. For instance, we can work on aspects like substance use, poor sleep, unhealthy relationships, and unmanaged ADHD symptoms.

- Some risk factors are not within our control. Genetic predisposition, chronic illness, and traumatic experiences are things that happen to us, and we must learn to deal with them in the aftermath.

While we can't change everything, we *can* take ownership of the parts we can influence. Managing these controllable risk factors strengthens our baseline of emotional resilience. One study has suggested that with the right support factors in place, life with ADHD can improve over time. The resilience factors identified were strategies to regulate ADHD symptoms, finding and maintaining supportive social relationships, societal and personal acceptance of neurodiversity, appreciating the positives of ADHD, and purposefully prioritizing meaningful activities in work and leisure (Dangmann et al., 2024).

Building Protective Factors: Your Personal Armor

Here are some evidence-based protective factors (Richard, 2022) that can buffer against the impact of stress and help regulate emotional intensity:

- **Build supportive relationships:** People who feel connected are more likely to regulate their emotions effectively. Whether it's a friend, therapist, support group, or mentor, social connection lowers stress and improves perspective.

  - **Action tip:** Schedule regular check-ins with someone who helps you feel grounded.

- **Practice self-compassion:** Self-blame after a rage episode only reinforces shame or regret. Instead, talk to yourself as you would a close friend.

  - **Ask:** "What would I say to someone I care about if they were struggling like this?"

- **Strengthen positive belief systems:** Optimism isn't blind positivity. It's the belief that while things are hard, you can face them. A proven tool is the "3-3-3 exercise," which can rewire your brain toward positive affect and motivation. Start by writing down

    - three things you're proud of yourself for.

    - three things you're grateful for.

    - three things you're looking forward to.

- **Develop problem-solving skills:** Reacting with rage often comes from feeling helpless. Resilient individuals ask, "What are my options?"

    - Practice breaking down problems into smaller steps and brainstorming at least two solutions. Even imperfect solutions can be better than no solutions.

- **Set boundaries:** Boundaries are essential to emotional well-being. Learning to say "no," advocate for your needs, or walk away from toxic dynamics can significantly reduce chronic anger triggers.

    - **Tip:** Write down three situations where you could start setting clearer boundaries.

Next, we will also look at how you can slowly help increase your frustration threshold or tolerance.

Building Frustration Tolerance: Exposure With Awareness

In ADHD, rage can be amplified by low frustration tolerance, a quick emotional "snap" at even mild irritations. One way to build tolerance is through gradual exposure to small triggers while practicing calm coping responses.

Example: If waiting in line is a trigger, deliberately practice it with a focus on slow breathing and mindful self-talk.

This teaches your nervous system that frustration is uncomfortable, but not dangerous, and that you are capable of tolerating it.

Reframing Triggers as Moments of Choice

A trigger doesn't have to lead to an outburst. It can be a pivot point or an opportunity to choose how you respond.

Tip: Slow down. Breathe. Remind yourself, "This is a choice point, not a command."

Over time, these moments of choice will rewire your brain's default responses.

Managing Stress: Healthy Outlets and Problem-Solving

Chronic stress increases irritability and impulsivity. Resilient people learn to process stress instead of suppressing it. Some effective strategies include

- physical activities, such as even 10 minutes of walking.

- creative expression via art, journaling, music, or a hobby you enjoy.

- talking to a trusted person.

- structured routines, which are especially helpful for ADHD brains. These could include sleeping and waking up at fixed times, or eating healthy meals three times a day, and so on.

Also, instead of ruminating on what's wrong, redirect focus to what's solvable. Even small problem-solving actions can restore a sense of agency.

Focus on What You Can Control

Control is calming. When overwhelmed, ask, "What's one thing I can change or influence in this situation?"

This might mean changing your environment, your response, or your interpretation, but no matter what, it works to break the cycle of helplessness.

Believe Change Is Possible, Even Without Motivation

For any change to stick, you need to believe that change is possible, necessary, and worth the effort. A powerful myth is that change requires motivation all the time. In reality, action often precedes motivation. Many resilient individuals simply commit to their routines on the hard days, even when they don't feel like it.

You don't need to feel inspired to do the right thing. You just need to do it.

This "showing up" builds confidence, control, and long-term change.

Long-Term Thinking: Play the Long Game

ADHD can be a condition of *now*, but resilience requires thinking beyond the moment. It becomes important to ask yourself the following:

- What's the long-term cost of reacting on impulse?

- What kind of person do I want to become?

- What legacy do I want to leave with my behavior?

Long-term thinking is a resilience skill, shifting your compass from short-term emotion to lasting purpose.

Ultimately, having emotional resilience isn't about being unaffected, but rather becoming stronger through the storm.

With each challenge, you will gain more insight, skill, and the ability to respond rather than react. You're not broken; you're building.

Key Takeaways

In this chapter, we looked at ways to reframe impulsive thoughts as moments of pause.

In the next chapter, we will continue to explore more practical ways of grounding oneself in the face of rage.

Self Reflection

- What does resilience mean to me, and how have I bounced back before?

- What stressors are within my control to change? Who supports me, and how can I build stronger connections?

- How do I speak to myself after I lose control—can I be kinder?

- What healthy ways can I manage stress this week?

- What boundaries do I need to set?

- Can I take one helpful action today, even without motivation?

- Who do I want to become, and what's one step closer to that vision?

Chapter 11

Practical Exercises—
Grounding Techniques and
Cognitive Reframing

The onset of ADHD-related rage can feel sudden, fast, overwhelming, and hard to control. However, like any skill, emotional regulation can be learned and improved through practice. This chapter provides actionable exercises designed to help you take control in the heat of the moment. With consistency, these strategies can help you interrupt the automatic cycle of anger and build more constructive responses.

Grounding Exercises: Quick Techniques to Regain Control

Grounding exercises bring you back to the present moment, helping you shift from a reactive state into awareness.

Box Breathing

This is a four-step breathing method that calms the nervous system.

How to do it:

- Inhale for four counts.

- Hold for four counts.

- Exhale for four counts.

- Hold for four counts.

Repeat this for 3–5 minutes or until you feel your body start to relax.

This exercise activates the parasympathetic nervous system, reducing the intensity of anger and panic.

Object-Focused Grounding

This exercise helps you anchor your attention by fully engaging with a single object in your environment.

How to do it:

- Look around and pick any object near you—it could be a pen, a coffee mug, a plant, or even a piece of clothing you're wearing.

- Focus all your attention on that object.

- Notice its color, texture, shape, and details like scratches, patterns, or how the light reflects off it.

- If you're holding it, pay attention to how it feels in your hand—cool, warm, rough, soft, heavy, or light.

- Keep your attention on that object for at least one full minute.

- As other thoughts come up, gently return your focus to the object, not by force, but as gently as guiding a curious mind back to a task.

This is a low-effort yet highly effective way to divert your brain from escalating anger. It gives your ADHD mind something tangible to concentrate on without feeling like a chore or countdown. It also trains attention gently, building self-regulation over time.

Rapid Body Scan

Quickly check in with different parts of your body, from head to toe.

Steps:

- Close your eyes and scan your body.

- Notice where you're holding tension (jaw, fists, shoulders, etc.).

- Breathe into those areas and gently release the tension.

Tension often mirrors internal emotional states. Releasing it physically can signal the brain that it's safe to calm down.

Slowing Down Through Enjoyable Activities

Anger often thrives in urgency and pressure. Slowing down helps disrupt that pace.

Engage in a Hobby

When you feel the pressure building, shift your focus to something enjoyable or some simple routine. This might be drawing, solving a puzzle, knitting, organizing a drawer, or even watering plants.

ADHD brains often benefit from task-switching, especially to something low-stakes. It gives your mind a chance to self-regulate and process feelings indirectly.

Journaling for Emotional Clarity

If you struggle with verbal expression or fear saying something you'll regret, writing can be your outlet.

Freewriting Exercise

Set a timer for five minutes and write whatever comes to mind. Don't worry about grammar or structure. Just let your thoughts spill.

Prompt ideas:

- "What am I really feeling beneath the anger?"

- "What triggered this emotion?"

- "What do I need right now?"

Writing slows down reactive thoughts and allows for clarity. It can also prevent you from bottling things up.

Don't Avoid—Pause and Revisit

Avoidance can make small issues grow into big ones. Instead, take a break and come back with a clearer mind.

The "Cool-Down and Return" Technique

1. **Acknowledge the conflict:** "I'm upset right now. I need time."

2. **Step away:** Use one of the grounding or slowing exercises.

3. **Set a time to revisit the issue:** "I'll come back to this in 30 minutes."

4. **Return and express your thoughts calmly:** You can use your journaled notes as a guide.

When you do the above, you're not running away; you're regulating first, then communicating more effectively.

Behavior Logs

Understanding your anger patterns helps you gain long-term control.

How to Track:

- What happened? (situation/context)

- What did I feel? (emotions)

- What did I do? (response)

- What was the result? (consequence)

- What could I try next time? (reflection)

Regular logging can highlight specific triggers and show you progress over time.

Digital Tools for Daily Support

There are a variety of ADHD-focused apps and digital tools that can help you stay organized and reduce frustration triggers.

App Features to Look For:

- task checklists (e.g., Todoist, TickTick)

- emotional tracking (e.g., Daylio, Moodnotes)

- reminders for breaks and cool-downs

- journaling or note sections for quick logging

Tools like these can reduce the mental load, which is a common source of irritability in ADHD.

Visual Aids for Clarity and Control

Create or use visual reminders of your goals and progress.

Ideas:

- emotion wheel or color-coded rage scale (e.g., Green = calm, Red = meltdown)

- anger tool kit poster (with your favorite calming techniques)

- daily progress chart (track days with successful cool-downs or regulated responses)

ADHD brains often respond well to visual cues. These tools provide quick references and reinforce positive habits.

Cognitive Restructuring: Challenging Thoughts That Fuel Anger

Sometimes the problem lies not in the situation, but in the story you tell yourself. When you're dealing with ADHD, anger often gets amplified by black-and-white thinking, internal criticism, and old patterns of frustration.

Shift the Story

Start by identifying the thought that triggered your emotional spiral. Then, challenge and reframe it.

Step-by-step:

- **Write down the triggering thought.**

  - **Example:** "They're ignoring me on purpose. No one respects me."

- **Ask yourself:**

  - Is this 100% true?

  - What else could be going on?

- What would I say to a friend in this situation?

- **Neutral reframe:** "Maybe they're overwhelmed too and didn't notice."

- **Positive affirmation:** "My value doesn't depend on how others respond. I can choose to communicate clearly and calmly."

It trains your brain to interrupt the inner critic and replace reactionary thoughts with grounded, flexible thinking.

Self-Compassion: Kindness Toward Yourself in the Midst of Struggle

ADHD can make everyday situations feel harder than they need to be. It's easy to turn that frustration inward. Practicing self-compassion helps break the cycle of shame and anger.

The Self-Compassion Pause

When you notice self-critical thoughts surfacing, try this quick intervention:

- **Notice the judgment.**

  - **Example:** "I always screw things up."

- **Replace it with concern and care.**

  - "This is a tough moment. I'm struggling, and that's okay."

- **Bring in kindness.**

  - "What do I need right now? Rest? Clarity? A moment to breathe?"

Self-compassion isn't letting yourself off the hook—it's giving yourself what you need to try again without spiraling into rage or defeat.

You're Not Alone: Common Humanity vs Isolation

Anger often breeds isolation. It makes you feel like you're the only one losing it, or you're too much. The truth is, you're not alone.

Mindful Connection Exercise

Take a moment to reflect on this truth: *Everyone struggles. Everyone reacts sometimes in ways they regret.*

Write a short paragraph or even just a few lines beginning with,

- "I'm not the only one who feels this way..."

- "It's human to get overwhelmed..."

- "Others are fighting battles I can't see..."

Reconnecting with your common humanity shrinks shame and fosters empathy—for yourself and others.

Mindfulness vs Rumination

Rumination is replaying the same angry scene over and over. Mindfulness is noticing that you're stuck and gently stepping out of it.

The Thought Train

Picture yourself standing on the platform as your thoughts as a train passes by.

- When you catch yourself ruminating, say: "That's just a thought train. I don't have to get on."

- Bring your focus back to your breath, your body, or your surroundings.

This builds the capacity to not engage with thoughts that spiral deeper into anger.

Behavioral Tracking: Know Your Patterns to Change Them

Tracking your reactions gives you insight. Insight gives you power.

Exercise: Reaction Journal

Each time you experience anger, jot down answers to the following:

- What happened?

- How did I react (words, tone, body language)?

- What was the result?

- What could I do differently next time?

Communication Pattern Rewire

Understand the four main communication styles:

- **Aggressive:** Attacking or dominating others.

- **Passive:** Avoiding conflict and staying silent even when you're unhappy about the situation.

- **Passive-aggressive:** Indirect resistance or sarcasm against others.

- **Assertive:** Clear, respectful, honest communication with people.

Pick a recent situation where you responded in a way you weren't proud of. Now, rewrite your response in an assertive tone:

- "Here's how I felt..."

- "Here's what I needed..."

- "Can we find a way to solve this?"

Most conflict escalates due to *how* we communicate, not just *what* we say. Being assertive reduces misunderstandings and earns respect.

Trigger Identification and Exposure: Be in Charge of Yourself

Avoiding your triggers can seem helpful short-term, but it reinforces fear. Gradual, mindful exposure helps you stay calm even when exposed to tough situations.

Trigger Map

1. **List your common anger triggers,** both internal (thoughts like "I'm failing again") and external (interruptions, noise, lateness).

2. **Rank them** from "mildly irritating" to "rage-inducing."

3. Start exposing yourself gently to the lower-ranked ones while practicing your calming tools. Celebrate each time you stay grounded.

This exercise helps you build emotional stamina. With practice, you'll feel more in charge—even when facing difficult situations.

Creating a Personal Toolbox: Your Go-To Strategy Kit

Keep in mind that not every tool will fit your disposition or situation. Your goal is to create a personalized plan you can rely on when anger spikes.

Build Your Toolbox

Pick your favorite strategies from this chapter and answer the following:

Impulse and Fire

- What works best for me when I'm overwhelmed?

- What calms my body quickly?

- What clears my mind?

- What helps me express myself instead of exploding or shutting down?

Example Go-To Strategy:

Name: The Reset Plan

When I feel rage building up, I will do as follows:

1. Step away and do a body scan or breathwork.

2. Write down what I'm feeling (or record a voice note).

3. Revisit the issue when I'm calm.

4. Use my communication script to talk it through.

You may not be able to "fix" yourself, but personalizing the strategies above to work for you will help you know yourself, respect your limits, and equip yourself with tools to handle life with more confidence and calm.

These exercises won't eliminate rage overnight, but they will help you build awareness, slow down impulsivity, and express yourself with more clarity and control. You can think of each exercise as a weight you're lifting to strengthen your emotional resilience. The more you practice, the stronger and more in control you'll become.

While consistently practising each of the above, you don't need a perfect record, only a system that works *most* of the time. These exercises won't change your neurology, but they will strengthen your ability to meet anger with awareness, choice, and compassion.

Key Takeaways

This chapter has explored a variety of tools, which can be exercised in a moment of rage as well as interwoven into one's schedule to help with anger management.

Chapter 12

A Lifetime of Calm—Creating a Personal Plan for Anger Management and ADHD

Jason, a 38-year-old construction site supervisor, used to be known for his temper. A delayed delivery, miscommunication with workers, or unexpected changes in plans would drive his anger into shouting matches and slammed tools. His crew respected his skills but was often intimidated by his aggressive bouts.

After a heated argument nearly cost him a long-term contract, Jason realized something had to change. He sought professional help and was diagnosed with ADHD. Through therapy and coaching, he learned how impulsivity and emotional dysregulation were driving his anger. He started practicing mindfulness, journaling, and using practical strategies like breaking large projects into smaller, time-blocked steps.

Now, when things don't go as planned, as they often don't in construction, Jason takes a pause. Instead of yelling, he steps away, breathes deeply, and regroups. He keeps a stress ball in his pocket and uses checklists to stay focused. If a worker makes a mistake, he addresses it calmly and constructively.

His team notices he's more patient and easier to talk to. He still feels frustration, but instead of blowing up, he channels it into problem-solving. He realizes that he's not perfect, but he's in control, and the worksite runs smoother because of it.

What does anger management look like? Does it mean you will no longer feel angry? Of course not. Anger is a part of being human, and with ADHD, it may still surface. However, learning to manage it gives you power. You'll interact more effectively, feel more confident, and live with far less regret and tension. With that in mind, let's look at ways to sustain anger management and control techniques so that they become a part of you for the long haul.

Building Consistency

Anger management isn't a one-time fix; it's constantly building sustainable habits that help you stay grounded, especially in a world where stress comes at you from all directions. Consistency is the foundation. To start, let's look at how stress affects different parts of your life and how to begin managing it intentionally.

Stress Self-Assessment Exercise

Rate your current stress levels in the following areas on a scale of 0–10, where 0 is no stress and 10 is extreme stress:

- work or school responsibilities

- family and home life

- financial situation

- personal health (physical and mental)

- time management

- social relationships and support

- sleep and rest

- future planning or uncertainty

Once you've scored each area, look at the ones with the highest stress levels. Ask yourself: *Which of these are within my control right now?* For example, you may not be able to control the demands of your job entirely, but you can improve how you respond to them. You may be able to set clearer boundaries, delegate tasks, or get better rest.

Tailor your action strategy: Choose one or two areas where you scored high and write down 2–3 specific actions you can take. For instance,

- if you scored high in time management, try using a planner or digital calendar to block out tasks.

- if finances are a stressor, create a simple monthly budget and track your spending.

- if relationships are strained, schedule regular check-ins or practice calm communication strategies.

Track your progress: Revisit this exercise every two weeks. Now, think carefully about the following questions: Are your scores improving? Are your strategies helping? If you feel there is no improvement, you need to adjust your strategies. As always, the goal isn't perfection, but progress. The more consistently you practice the above steps, the more control you'll gain over your reactions, stress, and ultimately, even anger.

Monitoring Progress

Growth is not always loud or dramatic. In fact, it's often quiet, slow, and personal. When managing ADHD-related anger, tracking your progress helps reinforce change and build motivation.

The SMART goal framework is a great way to set clear, realistic objectives.

SMART stands for the following:

- **Specific:** What exactly do you want to change?

- **Measurable:** How will you track your progress?

- **Achievable:** Is the target realistic based on your current capacity?

- **Relevant:** Does it align with your bigger emotional goals?

- **Time-bound:** Set a timeframe for work.

Example Goal:

"For the next two weeks, I will use a breathing technique or take a short walk whenever I feel overwhelmed at work, and record how many times I successfully pause before reacting."

Each time you respond calmly rather than reacting in anger, write it down. These notes are your personal wins. They might look as small as "Didn't shout when plans changed" or "Paused and asked for clarification instead of snapping," but they count.

Apart from SMART goals, another powerful and ADHD-friendly framework for goal setting and tracking is the WOOP method (Cousins, 2024), which stands for the following:

- **Wish:** What do you want to achieve?

  - **Example:** "I want to respond calmly when I feel triggered instead of yelling."

- **Outcome:** What would the best result feel like?

  - **Example:** "I'll feel proud, in control, and my relationships will improve."

- **Obstacle:** What internal habit or feeling gets in the way?

  - **Example:** "I feel overwhelmed too quickly and react without thinking."

- **Plan:** What can you do when the obstacle arises? Use an **If–Then** plan.

  - **Example:** "If I feel overwhelmed, then I will count to 10 and take a deep breath before responding."

WOOP is especially helpful for people with ADHD because of its emotionally engaging, visual, and action-oriented method, helping bridge the gap between intention and follow-through. It is also effective because it focuses on visualizing success and confronting obstacles, instead of just goal-setting in a vacuum. It helps you prepare for emotional triggers by anticipating real challenges. The "if–then" planning supports impulsivity control by preloading an alternative action.

WOOP can be revisited weekly or even daily to adjust goals and keep progress aligned with your emotional and behavioral patterns.

Once you decide on a goal-setting framework and use it over a few weeks, remember to look back and ask yourself these questions:

- Are there fewer outbursts?

- Do I feel more in control in situations that used to trigger me?

- Am I catching myself before I spiral?

Then do the "Old You versus New You" exercise. On one side of a page, describe how you used to respond to stress and frustration. On the other side, describe what's different now.

How does this shift make you feel? More grounded? More respected? Proud?

You may not have eliminated anger, but you've transformed your relationship with it, and the real progress is in moving from reaction to reflection, as well as from chaos to clarity.

A Commitment to Growth

You've made it to the end of this journey—but in truth, this is only the beginning. Managing ADHD-related anger isn't a straight road. It's a lifelong commitment to self-awareness, self-regulation, and meaningful change. Let's recap the action steps that lay the foundation for your long-term success:

- **Self-awareness and tracking:** You notice your triggers, whether it's a missed deadline, a loud environment, or feeling misunderstood. Journaling or mood tracking helps you catch patterns and gain clarity about what fuels your emotional responses.

- **Managing emotional regulation:** You practice pausing. You learn to breathe, shake off the tension, stop, and sense what's going on in your body before it erupts into anger. These tools help you gain control one moment at a time.

- **ADHD-specific coping strategies:** You learn to structure your chaos. Techniques like the STOP method, timers, breaking down tasks, and reducing cognitive overload. These strategies support your brain to work with you, not against you.

- **Developing communication and boundaries:** You've shifted from blame to assertiveness, using "I feel" statements and learning to step away when needed. You asked for support and communicated your goals.

- **Addressing the root causes:** You acknowledge the biological roots of ADHD. You continue to explore therapy, sleep, nutrition, and potentially medication. You are taking ownership of your well-being.

- **Measuring progress and practicing self-compassion:** You set goals, track your wins, and recognize the truth that not everyone is obligated to stay while you heal. ADHD is never an excuse to continue with old patterns. It is a reason to try harder, understand yourself, and build systems that work. Even your best efforts may not fix everything, but effort, insight, and growth matter.

Repairing damaged relationships, staying emotionally present, and breaking old dynamics requires consistent attention. Remember that with patience, support, and self-care, progress is possible. Keep going, because you're worth the work!

Key Takeaways

To sum up, controlling one's rage is not out of anyone's grasp. It can be built with consistent efforts, constant monitoring, and the urge for personal and emotional growth.

Conclusion

By now, you've walked through scenarios that may have felt eerily familiar—sudden outbursts, misunderstood frustration, broken cycles of effort and relapse, the invisible weight of emotional dysregulation. If you saw yourself mirrored in these pages, know this: Your struggle is valid, your challenges are real, and most importantly, change is not only possible—it is already beginning.

Anger, when viewed through the ADHD lens, takes on new dimensions. It is not merely an emotion that erupts, but a complex interplay of neurobiology, trauma, triggers, and temperament. This book was not written to shame those outbursts or ask you to "just calm down." Instead, it was designed to guide you with empathy and science toward understanding, then regulating, and finally owning your emotional world.

Unfortunately, ADHD does not come with an off-switch for big feelings. However, with the tools outlined here—from mindfulness and cognitive behavioral frameworks to grounding exercises and trigger mapping—you now hold the tool kit to shape a different response, one of awareness over impulsivity, and strategy over shame.

It's also worth repeating that emotional regulation is a practice, not a personality trait. On some days, you will feel like you're backsliding. On others, you may surprise yourself with your newfound ability to pause. Let both kinds of days exist without judgment. ADHD brains are wired for intensity, and that intensity can become your superpower when you hone and not suppress it.

You may be undertaking this journey alongside therapy, medication, or a support system. Let these tools integrate with your larger healing strategy. If you're doing this on your own, let this book be a voice reminding you that you are not alone and that you are not broken. If you want to explore more resources for anger management or impulse control, you can always head out to the courses on impulsivity.com as well.

You've examined how trauma, neurotransmitters, executive dysfunction, and hypersensitivity all contribute to the way your brain handles stress. You've learned how anger is often a secondary emotion—your brain's last-ditch effort to cope when it feels overwhelmed, unsafe, unheard. The science is now yours. The practical methods are now yours. The responsibility to implement them rests with you, but so does the power.

Remember, real change isn't loud. There might not be grand announcements or public victories. It happens in a single moment of choosing to breathe before you speak, in a small decision to walk away rather than escalate, and in tracking a trigger and meeting it with curiosity rather than contempt. Don't count these as small wins; they are seismic shifts.

This is not the end of your story. In fact, it's the first chapter where *you* start writing the plot. Take what you've learned here and make it yours. You may still feel overwhelmed. You may still face outbursts. But now, you know why. And now, you know what to do next.

Stay committed. Stay curious. Stay kind—to others, yes, but especially to yourself.

You're doing the work. And that's more than enough.

Glossary

ADHD (attention deficit hyperactivity disorder): A neurodevelopmental disorder characterized by inattention, hyperactivity, and impulsivity, often leading to emotional dysregulation and executive function challenges.

Amygdala: A brain region responsible for processing emotions (e.g., fear, anger). Overactivity here is linked to intense emotional reactions in ADHD.

Anger cycle: A recurring pattern where ADHD-related impulsivity and emotional dysregulation fuel anger outbursts, creating a self-perpetuating loop.

Anterior cingulate cortex (ACC): A brain area involved in decision-making and emotional regulation; mindfulness practices can enhance its function.

Basal ganglia: Brain structures that regulate motor control, emotions, and executive functions; often structurally different in ADHD brains.

Behavioral tracking: Monitoring reactions to identify triggers and patterns, often used in CBT to manage ADHD-related anger.

Cognitive behavioral therapy (CBT): A therapeutic approach that helps reframe negative thought patterns and behaviors, commonly used for ADHD and anger management.

Cognitive distortions: Irrational thought patterns (e.g., catastrophizing, black-and-white thinking) that exacerbate anger and low self-esteem in ADHD.

Cortisol: The "stress hormone" released during anger; ADHD brains may have atypical cortisol responses to stressors.

DBT (dialectical behavior therapy): A therapy combining mindfulness and emotional regulation skills to manage impulsivity and anger in ADHD.

Default mode network (DMN): Brain network active during rest; overactivity in ADHD is linked to rumination. Mindfulness can help regulate it.

Dopamine: A neurotransmitter tied to reward and motivation; low levels in ADHD contribute to impulsivity and emotional dysregulation.

Dysregulation (emotional): Difficulty managing emotional intensity, common in ADHD, leading to rapid mood shifts and anger outbursts.

Executive functioning: Cognitive skills (e.g., planning, impulse control) governed by the frontal lobe; impaired in ADHD.

Emotional flooding: Overwhelming, uncontrollable emotions (e.g., rage) due to ADHD-related sensory or cognitive overload.

Frontal cortex: The brain region managing impulse control and decision-making; often underactive in ADHD.

Fight-or-flight response: A primal reaction to stress, triggered by adrenaline and cortisol, often dysregulated in ADHD anger.

Hyperfocus: An ADHD trait of intense concentration on stimulating tasks, sometimes leading to neglect of other responsibilities.

Hypersensitivity: Heightened sensory or emotional reactions to stimuli (e.g., noise, criticism), common in ADHD.

Impulsivity: Acting without forethought, a core ADHD symptom that fuels anger outbursts and risky behaviors.

Interpersonal effectiveness: A DBT skill focusing on communication and relationship repair, crucial for ADHD-related social friction.

Limbic system: Brain structures governing emotions and motivation; ADHD can alter its function, increasing emotional reactivity.

Mindfulness: A practice of present-moment awareness, used to reduce ADHD-related impulsivity and emotional dysregulation.

Neurofeedback: A therapy using real-time brain activity monitoring to train self-regulation, sometimes used for ADHD.

Neurotransmitters: Chemical messengers (e.g., dopamine, norepinephrine) that are imbalanced in ADHD, affecting mood and focus.

Non-stimulants: Medication used for ADHD (e.g., atomoxetine) that work by targeting the neurotransmitter norepinephrine. They take longer to start working compared to stimulants.

Rejection-sensitive dysphoria (RSD): Extreme emotional pain triggered by perceived rejection, often comorbid with ADHD.

Rumination: Repetitive negative thinking, common in ADHD, worsening anger and depression.

Sensory overload: Overstimulation from environmental triggers (e.g., noise, lights), exacerbating ADHD emotional dysregulation.

Stimulants: ADHD medicines (e.g., methylphenidate) that boost dopamine/norepinephrine to improve focus and impulse control.

Triggers: Situations or stimuli (e.g., frustration, criticism) that provoke ADHD-related anger; identifying them is key to management.

About the Author

Dr. Yuliya Richard is a clinical psychologist who has nearly 20 years of experience in the field of impulse control disorders and their impact on human relationships. She currently works in a private practice in Sydney.

After researching dysfunctional impulsivity as part of her doctoral thesis, Dr. Richard founded the Impulsivity Project in 2015. An online program, Impulsivity targets recognizing, managing, and overcoming impulsive behaviors. It offers several courses for people who feel their personal or professional lives are out of balance, so they can establish a sense of control over themselves. Her clients include those who want to change or control their destructive urges, as well as those who have been hurt repeatedly by harmful impulsive behavior patterns. The courses on Impulsivity.com focus on thrust areas such as anger management, binge drinking, binge eating, overspending, procrastination, relationship rebuilding, and more.

References

1. Abdelnour, E., Jansen, M. O., & Gold, J. A. (2022). ADHD diagnostic trends: Increased recognition or overdiagnosis?. *Missouri Medicine*, *119*(5), 467–473. https://pmc.ncbi.nlm.nih.gov/articles/PMC9616454/#:~:text=Attention%20Deficit%20Hyperactivity%20Disorder%3A%20The

2. *ADHD alternative treatments.* (2025, January 15). WebMD. https://www.webmd.com/add-adhd/childhood-adhd/adhd-alternative-treatments

3. *ADHD and complementary health approaches.* (2023, August). NCCIH Clinical Digest for Health Professionals; NIH. https://www.nccih.nih.gov/health/providers/digest/adhd-and-complementary-health-approaches

4. *ADHD medications: How they work & side effects.* (2022, October 6). Cleveland Clinic. https://my.clevelandclinic.org/health/treatments/11766-adhd-medication

5. Albajara Sáenz, A., Villemonteix, T., & Massat, I. (2018). Structural and functional neuroimaging in attention-deficit/hyperactivity disorder. *Developmental Medicine & Child Neurology*, *61*(4), 399–405. https://doi.org/10.1111/dmcn.14050

6. Alternative treatments for attention deficit hyperactivity disorder. (2003). *Paediatrics & child health, 8*(4), 243–246. https://doi.org/10.1093/pch/8.4.243

7. American Heart Association. (2020, February 4). *Chronic stress can cause heart trouble.* American Heart Association. https://www.heart.org/en/news/2020/02/04/chronic-stress-can-cause-heart-trouble

8. Arnsten A. F. (2009). The emerging neurobiology of Attention Deficit Hyperactivity Disorder: The key Role of the prefrontal association cortex. *The Journal of Pediatrics, 154*(5), I–S43. https://doi.org/10.1016/j.jpeds.2009.01.018

9. *Art therapy in the treatment of attention deficit hyperactivity disorder: A scoping review of current applications.* (2021). [Master's thesis]. University of Adelaide. https://digital.library.adelaide.edu.au/server/api/core/bitstreams/13398000-568a-4b35-afc1-8f1a5e0a9120/content

10. Basiri, N. (2025). The effects of dialectical behavioural therapy (DBT) on cognitive and emotional symptoms of adult ADHD: A randomised pilot study. *Counselling and Psychotherapy Research, 25*(1). https://doi.org/10.1002/capr.12900

11. Beheshti, A., Chavanon, M. L., & Christiansen, H. (2020). Emotion dysregulation in adults with attention deficit hyperactivity disorder: a meta-analysis. *BMC Psychiatry, 20*(1), 120. https://doi.org/10.1186/s12888-020-2442-7

12. Blum, K., Chen, A. L., Braverman, E. R., Comings, D. E., Chen, T. J., Arcuri, V., Blum, S. H., Downs, B. W., Waite, R. L., Notaro, A., Lubar, J., Williams, L., Prihoda, T. J.,

Palomo, T., & Oscar-Berman, M. (2008). Attention-deficit-hyperactivity disorder and reward deficiency syndrome. *Neuropsychiatric disease and treatment*, 4(5), 893–918. https://doi.org/10.2147/ndt.s2627

13. Brach, T. (n.d.). *RAIN: Recognize, allow, investigate, nurture*. Tara Brach. https://www.tarabrach.com/rain/

14. Brown, A. P. (2024, February 5). *Self defeating behavior: ADHD pitfalls and fixes*. Www.additudemag. com. https://www.additudemag.com/self-defeating-behavior-adhd/

15. Brown, T. E. (2025, March 18). *Exaggerated emotions: How and why ADHD triggers intense feelings*. ADDitude. https://www.additudemag.com/slideshows/adhd-emotions-understanding-intense-feelings/?

16. Cherry, K. (2024, July 14). *The 6 types of basic emotions and their effect on human behavior*. Verywell Mind. https://www.verywellmind.com/an-overview-of-the-types-of-emotions-4163976

17. Cole, P., Weibel, S., Nicastro, R., Hasler, R., Dayer, A., Aubry, J.-M., Prada, P., & Perroud, N. (2016). CBT/DBT skills training for adults with attention deficit hyperactivity disorder (ADHD). *Psychiatria Danubina*, 28(Suppl. 1), 103–107. https://www.researchgate.net/publication/308606478_CBTDBT_skills_training_for_adults_with_attention_deficit_hyperactivity_disorder_ADHD

18. Corominas-Roso, M., Palomar, G., Ferrer, R., Real, A., Nogueira, M., Corrales, M., Casas, M., & Ramos-Quiroga, J. A. (2015). Cortisol response to stress in adults with attention deficit hyperactivity disorder. *The International Journal of Neuropsychopharmacology*, 18(9), pyv027. https://doi.org/10.1093/ijnp/pyv027

19. Cousins, R. (2024). *WOOP: The science-backed strategy for turning goals into reality.* Thriva. https://thriva.co/hub/behaviour-change/woop-strategy#practical-application

20. Cronkleton, E. (2021, August 13). *What are the differences between an ADHD brain and a neurotypical brain.* Medical News Today. https://www.medicalnewstoday.com/articles/adhd-brain-vs-normal-brain

21. Dangmann, C. R., Skogli, G. K. W., Holthe, M. E. G., Steffenak, A. K. M., & Andersen, P. N. (2024). Life gets better: Important resilience factors when growing up with ADHD. *Journal of Attention Disorders, 28(8),* 1198–1209. https://doi.org/10.1177/10870547241246645

22. de Water, E., Demurie, E., Mies, G. W., & Scheres, A. (2024). Temporal discounting in children and adolescents with and without attention-deficit/hyperactivity disorder: a comparison of four scoring methods. *Child Neuropsychology, 30(5),* 702–721. https://doi.org/10.1080/09297049.2023.2268768

23. Diamond A. (2013). Executive functions. *Annual Review of Psychology, 64,* 135–168. https://doi.org/10.1146/annurev-psych-113011-143750 Ekman, P. (2022). *The atlas of emotion.* The Ekmans' Atlas of Emotions. https://atlasofemotions.org/

24. Faraone, S. V., & Larsson, H. (2019). Genetics of attention deficit hyperactivity disorder. Molecular psychiatry, 24(4), 562–575. https://doi.org/10.1038/s41380-018-0070-0

25. Fuermaier, A. B., Tucha, L., Evans, B. L., Koerts, J., de Waard, D., Brookhuis, K., Aschenbrenner, S., Thome, J., Lange, K. W., & Tucha, O. (2017). Driving and attention

deficit hyperactivity disorder. *Journal of neural transmission (Vienna, Austria : 1996)*, 124(Suppl 1), 55–67. https://doi.org/10.1007/s00702-015-1465-6

26. Garcia, S. E., & Tully, E. C. (2020). Children's recognition of happy, sad, and angry facial expressions across emotive intensities. *Journal of Experimental Child Psychology*, 197, 104881. https://doi.org/10.1016/j.jecp.2020.104881

27. Giedd, J. N. (2019). The enigma of neuroimaging in ADHD. *American Journal of Psychiatry*, 176(7), 503–504. https://doi.org/10.1176/appi.ajp.2019.19050540

28. Gupta, S. (2023, November 20). *Coping with mood swings in ADHD*. Verywell Mind. https://www.verywellmind.com/mood-swings-in-adhd-symptoms-causes-and-coping-5223511

29. Halmøy, A., Ring, A. E., Gjestad, R., Møller, M., Ubostad, B., Lien, T., Munkhaugen, E. K., & Fredriksen, M. (2022). Dialectical behavioral therapy-based group treatment versus treatment as usual for adults with attention-deficit hyperactivity disorder: a multicenter randomized controlled trial. *BMC Psychiatry*, 22(1), 738. https://doi.org/10.1186/s12888-022-04356-6

30. Hartman, C. A., Rommelse, N., van der Klugt, C. L., Wanders, R. B. K., & Timmerman, M. E. (2019). Stress exposure and the course of ADHD from childhood to young adulthood: Comorbid severe emotion dysregulation or mood and anxiety problems. *Journal of Clinical Medicine*, 8(11), 1824. https://doi.org/10.3390/jcm8111824

31. Hotte-Meunier, A., Sarraf, L., Bougeard, A., Bernier, F., Voyer, C., Deng, J., El Asmar, S., Stamate, A. N., Corbière, M., Villotti, P., & Sauvé, G. (2024).

Strengths and challenges to embrace attention-deficit/hyperactivity disorder in employment—A systematic review. *Neurodiversity*, 2. https://doi.org/10.1177/27546330241287655

32. Ilagan, G. (2024, August 19). *Anger as a secondary emotion: What's important to know.* Manhattan Center for Cognitive Behavioral Therapy. https://manhattancbt.com/anger-secondary-emotion/

33. Kandeğer, A., Ünal, Ş. O., Ergün, M. T., & Ataşlar, E. Y. (2023). Excessive mind wandering, rumination, and mindfulness mediate the relationship between ADHD symptoms and anxiety and depression in adults with ADHD. *Clinical Psychology & Psychotherapy*, 31(1). https://doi.org/10.1002/cpp.2940

34. Kariž, B. (2003, March). Art therapy and ADHD. *1st Arts and Therapies World Congress.* https://www.researchgate.net/publication/267473163_ART_THERAPY_AND_ADHD

35. Kessler, R. C., Adler, L., Ames, M., Barkley, R. A., Birnbaum, H., Greenberg, P., Johnston, J. A., Spencer, T., & st ??n, T. B. (2005). The prevalence and effects of adult attention deficit/hyperactivity disorder on work performance in a nationally representative sample of workers. *Journal of Occupational and Environmental Medicine*, 47(6), 565–572. https://doi.org/10.1097/01.jom.0000166863.33541.39

36. Knouse, L. E., & Safren, S. A. (2010). Current status of cognitive behavioral therapy for adult attention-deficit hyperactivity disorder. *The Psychiatric clinics of North America*, 33(3), 497–509. https://doi.org/10.1016/j.psc.2010.04.001

37. Kofler, M. J., Singh, L. J., Soto, E. F., Chan, E. S. M., Miller, C. E., Harmon, S. L., & Spiegel, J. A. (2020). Working memory and short-term memory deficits in ADHD: A bifactor modeling approach. *Neuropsychology*, 34(6), 686–698. https://doi.org/10.1037/neu0000641

38. Kral, T. R. A., Schuyler, B. S., Mumford, J. A., Rosenkranz, M. A., Lutz, A., & Davidson, R. J. (2018). Impact of short- and long-term mindfulness meditation training on amygdala reactivity to emotional stimuli. *NeuroImage*, *181*, 301–313. https://doi.org/10.1016/j.neuroimage.2018.07.013

39. Lange, K. W., Reichl, S., Lange, K. M., Tucha, L., & Tucha, O. (2010). The history of attention deficit hyperactivity disorder. *Attention Deficit and Hyperactivity Disorders*, 2(4), 241–255. https://doi.org/10.1007/s12402-010-0045-8

40. Lin, P.-I., Weng Tong Wu, Enoch Kordjo Azasu, & Tsz Ying Wong. (2024). Pathway from attention-deficit/hyperactivity disorder to suicide/self-harm. *Psychiatry Research*, 115936–115936. https://doi.org/10.1016/j.psychres.2024.115936

41. Littman, E. (2025, March 25). *Never enough? Why ADHD brains crave stimulation*. ADDitude. https://www.additudemag.com/brain-stimulation-and-adhd-cravings-dependency-and-regulation/?srsltid=AfmBOorreyOOWidVxGdIlgVilTsksLoX3fbNIAHCQ9dqRKxm_uzzScuA

42. Lopez, P. L., Torrente, F. M., Ciapponi, A., Lischinsky, A. G., Cetkovich-Bakmas, M., Rojas, J. I., Romano, M., & Manes, F. F. (2018). Cognitive-behavioural interventions for attention deficit hyperactivity disorder (ADHD) in adults. *The Cochrane Database of Systematic Reviews*,

3(3), CD010840. https://doi.org/10.1002/14651858. CD010840.pub2

43. Lovering, N. (2022, April 27). *Can you be addicted to anger?* Psych Central. https://psychcentral.com/lib/is-anger-an-addiction#tips

44. Mae, A. (2023, November 13). *ADHD sensory overload: Causes, treatment, and more.* MedicalNewsToday. https://www.medicalnewstoday.com/articles/adhd-sensory-overload

45. Magnus, W., Nazir, S., Anilkumar, A. C., & Shaban, K. (2023, August 8). *Attention deficit hyperactivity disorder (ADHD).* PubMed; StatPearls Publishing. https://www.ncbi.nlm.nih.gov/books/NBK441838/

46. Malloy-Diniz, L., Fuentes, D., Leite, W. B., Correa, H., & Bechara, A. (2007). Impulsive behavior in adults with attention deficit/ hyperactivity disorder: Characterization of attentional, motor and cognitive impulsiveness. *Journal of the International Neuropsychological Society, 13*(04). https://doi.org/10.1017/s1355617707070889

47. Makris, N., Biederman, J., Valera, E. M., Bush, G., Kaiser, J., Kennedy, D. N., Caviness, V. S., Faraone, S. V., & Seidman, L. J. (2007). Cortical thinning of the attention and executive function networks in adults with attention-deficit/hyperactivity disorder. *Cerebral Cortex, 17*(6), 1364–1375. https://doi.org/10.1093/cercor/bhl047

48. Marchand W. R. (2014). Neural mechanisms of mindfulness and meditation: Evidence from neuroimaging studies. *World Journal of Radiology, 6*(7), 471–479. https://doi.org/10.4329/wjr.v6.i7.471

49. McIntyre, K. M., Mogle, J. A., Scodes, J. M., Pavlicova, M., Shapiro, P. A., Gorenstein, E. E., Tager, F. A., Monk, C., Almeida, D. M., & Sloan, R. P. (2019). Anger-reduction treatment reduces negative affect reactivity to daily stressors. *Journal of Consulting and Clinical Psychology*, 87(2), 141–150. https://doi.org/10.1037/ccp0000359

50. McMillen, M., Walker-Journey, J., & King, L. M. (2024, May 13). *ADHD medications and side effects.* WebMD. https://www.webmd.com/add-adhd/adhd-medication-chart

51. *Mindfulness.* (2022). American Psychological Association. https://www.apa.org/topics/mindfulness

52. Modesto-Lowe, V., Farahmand, P., Chaplin, M., & Sarro, L. (2015). Does mindfulness meditation improve attention in attention deficit hyperactivity disorder?. *World Journal of Psychiatry*, 5(4), 397–403. https://doi.org/10.5498/wjp.v5.i4.397

53. Murray, K. (2025, April 10). *Addiction and anger management.* AddictionCenter. https://www.addictioncenter.com/addiction/anger-management/

54. Nakashita, A. (2025). Is emotion dysregulation disorder-specific in ADHD? Exploring mechanisms linking ADHD traits and mental health. *Research Gate (Pre Print).* https://doi.org/10.31234/osf.io/5kbg2_v2

55. Nárai, Á., Hermann, P., Rádosi, A., Vakli, P., Weiss, B., Réthelyi, J. M., Bunford, N., & Vidnyánszky, Z. (2023). Amygdala volume is associated with ADHD risk and severity beyond comorbidities in adolescents: Clinical testing of brain chart reference standards. *Research on Child and Adolescent Psychopathology.* https://doi.org/10.1101/2023.09.17.23295664

56. National Center for PTSD. (2022). *Anger and trauma.* National Center for PTSD. https://www.ptsd.va.gov/understand/related/anger.asp

57. Navidad, A. (2023, September 7). *Marshmallow test experiment.* SimplyPsychology. https://www.simplypsychology.org/marshmallow-test.html

58. Nigg, J. (2025, March 18). *The ADHD-anger connection: New insights into emotional dysregulation and treatment considerations.* ADDitude. https://www.additudemag.com/anger-issues-adhd-emotional-dysregulation/

59. NIMH. (2021). *Attention-deficit/hyperactivity disorder in adults: What you need to know.* National Institute of Mental Health. https://www.nimh.nih.gov/health/publications/adhd-what-you-need-to-know

60. Park, J., Kitayama, S., Markus, H. R., Coe, C. L., Miyamoto, Y., Karasawa, M., Curhan, K. B., Love, G. D., Kawakami, N., Boylan, J. M., & Ryff, C. D. (2013). Social status and anger expression: the cultural moderation hypothesis. *Emotion,* 13(6), 1122–1131. https://doi.org/10.1037/a0034273

61. Posner, J. (2020, March 9). *Mapping the ADHD brain: MRI scans may unlock better treatment and even symptom prevention.* ADDitude. https://www.additudemag.com/brain-mri-scans-adhd-research/?src=embed_link

62. Ramsay, J. R. (2018, April 30). *DBT: The emotional control therapy you need now.* ADDitude. https://www.additudemag.com/dbt-for-adhd-dialectical-behavioral-therapy/?

63. Richard, Y. (2022, September 25). *Learn anger management strategies with our online course.* Impulsivity Project Online. https://impulsivity.com.au/curriculum/anger-management-course/

64. Richard, Y., Tazi, N., Frydecka, D., Hamid, M. S., & Moustafa, A. A. (2022). A systematic review of neural, cognitive, and clinical studies of anger and aggression. *Current Psychology*, 1–13. Advance online publication. https://doi.org/10.1007/s12144-022-03143-6

65. Rosier, T. (2024, September 6). *Self-Sabotage and ADHD: Are you your own worst enemy?* ADDitude. https://www.additudemag.com/self-sabotage-adhd/?

66. Rostain, A. L. (2025, April 17). *6 cognitive distortions that fuel anxiety in ADHD brains.* ADDitude. https://www.additudemag.com/slideshows/cognitive-distortions-anxiety-adhd/?

67. Saccaro, L. F., Schilliger, Z., Perroud, N., & Piguet, C. (2021). Inflammation, Anxiety, and Stress in Attention-Deficit/Hyperactivity Disorder. *Biomedicines*, 9(10), 1313. https://doi.org/10.3390/biomedicines9101313

68. Saline, S. (2022, May 2). *How stress and self-sabotage interfere with ADHD happiness.* Psychology Today. https://www.psychologytoday.com/us/blog/your-way-adhd/202205/how-stress-and-self-sabotage-interfere-adhd-happiness

69. Saline, S. (2024, September 1). *How to control your anger when ADHD emotional reactivity kicks in.* ADDitude. https://www.additudemag.com/how-to-control-anger-emotional-reactivity-adhd/?srsltid=AfmBOoqY8bRlHg99UaflqCbLfTuol-dDO0CJtmwW6X4ndVFotKW1Dwyw&utm_

70. Saylor, K. E., & Amann, B. H. (2016). Impulsive aggression as a comorbidity of attention-deficit/hyperactivity disorder in children and adolescents. *Journal of Child and Adolescent Psychopharmacology*, 26(1), 19–25. https://doi.org/10.1089/cap.2015.0126

71. Shaw, P., Stringaris, A., Nigg, J., & Leibenluft, E. (2014). Emotion dysregulation in attention deficit hyperactivity disorder. *The American Journal of Psychiatry*, 171(3), 276–293. https://doi.org/10.1176/appi.ajp.2013.13070966

72. Shayanfar, S. (2016). *Adolescents' negative emotion regulation in the context of peer interactions* [Master's thesis]. University of Calgary. PRISM repository. https://ucalgary.scholaris.ca/server/api/core/bitstreams/aa6727dc-d788-4c75-b863-f09911a73a5b/content

73. Soler-Gutiérrez, A. M., Pérez-González, J. C., & Mayas, J. (2023). Evidence of emotion dysregulation as a core symptom of adult ADHD: A systematic review. *PloS one*, *18*(1), e0280131. https://doi.org/10.1371/journal.pone.0280131

74. Sorin, R. (2003). Validating young children's feelings and experiences of fear. *Contemporary Issues in Early Childhood*, 4(1), 80–89. https://doi.org/10.2304/ciec.2003.4.1.8

75. Sudre, G., Szekely, E., Sharp, W., Kasparek, S., & Shaw, P. (2017). Multimodal mapping of the brain's functional connectivity and the adult outcome of attention deficit hyperactivity disorder. *Proceedings of the National Academy of Sciences of the United States of America*, 114(44), 11787–11792. https://doi.org/10.1073/pnas.1705229114

76. Suman. (2016). Anger expression: A study on gender differences. *International Journal of Indian Psychology, 3*(4). https://doi.org/10.25215/0304.140

77. Sutton, J. (2019, April 9). *What is mindfulness? Definition + benefits (incl. psychology).* PositivePsychology.com. https://positivepsychology.com/what-is-mindfulness/

78. Tang, Y.-Y. (2017). *The neuroscience of mindfulness meditation.* Springer International Publishing. https://doi.org/10.1007/978-3-319-46322-3

79. Toohey, M. J. (2021). Cognitive behavioral therapy for anger management. In A. Wenzel (Ed.), *Handbook of cognitive behavioral therapy: Applications* (pp. 331–359). American Psychological Association. https://doi.org/10.1037/0000219-010

80. *Unmasking cognitive distortions in ADHD: Strategies for a balanced mind.* (2025, May 3). Focusbear. https://www.focusbear.io/blog-post/unmasking-cognitive-distortions-in-adhd-strategies-for-a-balanced-mind

81. Vanta, B. (2024, September 9). *Physiology of anger.* MentalHealth. https://www.mentalhealth.com/library/handling-anger-management-relapses

82. Viering, T., Naaijen, J., van Rooij, D., Thiel, C., Philipsen, A., Dietrich, A., Franke, B., Buitelaar, J., & Hoekstra, P. J. (2021). Amygdala reactivity and ventromedial prefrontal cortex coupling in the processing of emotional face stimuli in attention-deficit/hyperactivity disorder. *European Child & Adolescent Psychiatry, 31*(12), 1895–1907. https://doi.org/10.1007/s00787-021-01809-3

83. Wadley, J. (2018, October 9). *Thinking outside the box: Adults with ADHD not constrained in creativity.* University

of Michigan News. https://news.umich.edu/thinking-outside-the-box-adults-with-adhd-not-constrained-in-creativity/

84. Wang, F. (n.d.). *Neuroscience of mindfulness meditation.* Wharton Neuroscience Initiative. https://neuro.wharton.upenn.edu/community/winss_scholar_blog2/

85. What is cognitive behavioral therapy? (2017). *American Psychological Association.* https://www.apa.org/ptsd-guideline/patients-and-families/cognitive-behavioral

86. White, M. (n.d.). *Complementary and alternative treatment of ADHD.* UC Davis Health | MIND Institute. https://health.ucdavis.edu/mind-institute/resources/understanding-adhd/adhd-cam-treatments

87. *Why are my feelings so intense? Emotional flooding and the ADHD brain.* (2024, September 27). ADDept. https://www.addept.org/living-with-adult-add-adhd/why-are-my-feelings-so-intense

88. Yusuf Ali, A., Inyang, B., Koshy, F. S., George, K., Poudel, P., Chalasani, R., Goonathilake, M. R., Waqar, S., George, S., Jean-Baptiste, W., & Mohammed, L. (2022). Elements that influence the development of Attention Deficit Hyperactivity Disorder (ADHD) in children. *Cureus, 14*(8), e27835. https://doi.org/10.7759/cureus.27835